New Directions in Religious Education

Finola Cunnane

for Anthony:
God's blessing on 'entering' Mater Dei
Fall 2005 **VERITAS**
Fr. bb

First published 2004 by
Veritas Publications
7/8 Lower Abbey Street
Dublin 1
Ireland
Email publications@veritas.ie
Website www.veritas.ie

ISBN 1 85390 772 3

Cover painting by Eugene D'Arcy
Cover design by Pierce Design
Printed in the Republic of Ireland by Betaprint Ltd., Dublin

*Veritas books are printed on paper made from the wood pulp of managed
forests. For every tree felled, at least one tree is planted, thereby renewing
natural resources.*

Dedicated to my first religious educators,
Gabriel and Mary,
and to the Sisters of St Louis
with whom I continue the conversation.

CONTENTS

Introduction   7

1   A Babel of Languages   17

2   Setting the Framework for the Conversation   36

3   A Paradigm Shift: Education –
    The Overall Framework   80

4   The Family as Religious Educator   98

5   The School as Religious Educator   123

6   The Parish as Religious Educator   146

    Epilogue: What Next?   183

    Notes   187

    Bibliography   201

INTRODUCTION

Religious education is undergoing dramatic challenges in many parts of the world today. The debates that arise from this situation highlight the confusion that results from the diversity in terminology, identity and purpose of religious education as it is experienced in its implementation. Such confusion has frequently led to inappropriate expectations on the part of educational bodies, Church personnel and society in general. The challenge facing us today concerns the lens through which we regard religious education. Is it a thing of the past or is it something whose time has not yet arrived? It is my conviction that religious education is one of the most important issues facing our world today. There is a need for a language that honours both the educational and the religious in life. The aim of this book is to provide food for thought and to suggest a new imagining of religious education. Perhaps as you read this book you, too, can join the conversation and help bring to birth some creative possibilities for religious education as, together, we unveil the truest meaning of this endeavour.

This book relies heavily on the work of Gabriel Moran, a prolific writer in the field of religion and education. Moran, the author of some twenty books and more than two hundred articles, has for over thirty years, noted the absence of a field of religious education, has sought to break open the meaning of words in order to bring about linguistic clarity and has called for an adequate theory of religious education. In order to get a manageable hold on the essence of his thought, I have chosen to work with three major themes in his work, themes that are more fitting for an educational framework for religious education. They are 1) the meaning and forms of education; 2) the meaning and forms of teaching and 3) moral education and educating morally. The synthesis of these themes is found in an education towards adulthood.

This book is divided into six major chapters. Chapter 1, 'A Babel of Languages', presents the current situation of religious education. Four major problems are isolated and addressed by exploring the concept of religious education through the lens of Gabriel Moran. Prior to outlining his conceptualisation of religious education, the first part of this chapter examines the positions of other leading scholars in the field. This paves the way for the remainder of the chapter to explore a richer meaning of religious education.

Chapter 2, 'Setting the Framework for the Conversation', presents three of the main themes pertinent for a fuller meaning and understanding of religious education: (1) the meaning and forms of education; (2) the meaning and forms of teaching and (3) moral education and educating morally.

(1) *Meaning and forms of education:* Airing his dissatisfaction with current educational language which narrowly perceives school as *the* form of education, Gabriel Moran acknowledges that there is no single meaning of education. In order to reclaim, reform, and restate the meaning of the term *education,* he calls for an examination of two key issues: (i) the etymology and history of the word and (ii) the inclusion of people rendered voiceless through their exclusion from its current meaning. This leads him to name education at the interplay of life forms and, thus, his meaning of education emerges. This meaning

comprises two forms of education – schooling and laboratory. The schooling part of laboratory takes place in an academic setting, while the non-schooling part comprises the life forms in which people are taught how to live – family, work, and leisure time.

(2) *Meaning and forms of teaching:* This theme comprehensively explores the meaning of the verb *to teach* and points to several forms of teaching, only one of which is schoolteaching. Teaching, according to Gabriel Moran, means *showing someone how to do something.* In its most complete expression, it means showing someone how to live and how to die. Human teaching, in this chapter, is explored by examining the way in which we teach by design. This is followed by differentiating between three groups or families of languages – homiletic, therapeutic, and academic – each of which takes place in different educational settings.

(3) *Moral education and educating morally:* The issue of moral education comes to the fore in any attempt to delineate a satisfactory meaning of religious education. In examining morality under the rubric of *moral education*, the history of the term is outlined and special attention given to the contributions of Durkheim, Piaget, Kohlberg, and Gilligan. Aware that Kohlberg's theory of moral development is at odds with religious and Christian education, Moran suggests three stages in the process of maturing morally: (i) uneducated morality; (ii) ethical thinking; and (iii) educational morality. The remainder of the chapter examines the meaning of teaching morally, teaching morality, and teaching morality (ethics) in classrooms.

These three themes point to the need for an educational system that is open to all people throughout their lives. This requires patterns of education that are inclusive of both children and adults. Education towards adulthood means structuring experiences that will guide people toward psychological, social and religious maturity. Adulthood is an ideal – an ideal sought after, but never fully acquired, throughout the lifespan.

The third chapter, 'A Paradigm Shift: Education – The Overall Framework', presents Moran's paradigmatic shift from an ecclesiastical language to an educational language. The ecclesiastical language proved to be unsatisfactory because of theology's control of catechetical language and content, with the result that catechetics became a kind of practical theology. Moran shifts to an educational language in an effort to open dialogue within and beyond the churches. This paradigmatic shift offers a second language in which to speak about religious education. Religious education now becomes the interplay of two complementary, but differing, aims: (1) to teach religion and (2) to teach to be religious. To teach religion involves the understanding of one's own religion, as well as the religion of others. To teach to be religious involves formation and nurturance in a way of life.

Chapters 4, 5 and 6 present the family, the school and the parish as educator. Using the three themes presented in Chapter 2 the author illustrates how the family, school and parish educates, teaches and educates morally. Chapter 4, 'The Family as Religious Educator', presents the family as educator, teacher and moral educator. Within the family, people are educated from the first moments of life. Parents and children are in a reciprocal educative relationship with the parents parenting the child and the child childing the parent. The three themes are presented as follows:

(1) *The family as educator*: The family is a compelling form of education. Being the main form of education for infants and young children, the family educates through its relation to the environment and especially through its relationship with non-familial forms of organisation. The family educates by being a

place of community, a place where both parents and children together learn the meaning of work, wisdom and knowledge.

(2) *The family as teacher*: This section of Chapter 4 illustrates how the family teaches by design and by example. The family teaches by showing members how to do something, how to live, and how to die. It teaches through its incorporation of the first and second languages of teaching – the homiletic and the therapeutic. In other words, it teaches through storytelling, through praise/condemn; welcome/thank; confess/forgive; mourn/comfort. Ultimately, it teaches how to be religious.

(3) *The Family as moral educator:* The intention here is to portray how authentic teaching always includes a moral dimension. The family educates morally all the time through modelling, witnessing and demonstrating a way of life. The family educates morally through care, attention, values, and attitude to life. It educates morally by being attentive to the various teaching forms available, as well as the languages of teaching appropriate to each form. It educates morally through its sharing of family stories, stories that are expressed through symbols, codes of behaviour, sense of humour, ways of dress and address, ways of sharing joy and sorrow. The moral life is taught by the family that has character and virtue.

In engaging in education, teaching and moral education, the final section of Chapter 4 examines the ways in which the family educates towards adulthood. Within the family, education towards adulthood takes place through intergenerational contact, through activities that are inclusive of both adults and children, activities that invite all to grow together towards a mature, wise and integral adulthood.

Chapter 5, 'The School as Religious Educator', presents the role of schooling and the school as agents of religious education. *The school as educator*: This section points to the fact that the school, as educator, needs to understand itself as only one form of education. Education is an interplay of life forms, only one of which is school. This form of education is not confined to people between five and eighteen years, but spans a person's life from birth to death.

(2) *The school as teacher*: School is a place where multiple forms of teaching and multiple languages of teaching take place. The third family of languages – academic – finds its particular place here through dramatic performance, dialectical discussion, and academic criticism. This third family of languages, with its concomitant forms of teaching is meant to complement, rather than replace, the homiletic and the therapeutic languages of teaching. School also has the responsibility to teach by design. While much indirect teaching occurs in the family and the parish community, the classroom in the school is the place for more intentional education. Schooling uses a particular design or designs in order to educate. The responsibility of the teacher is to work with the students and the environment in order to improve the existing educational design. Good teaching never severs its roots from the metaphor of design.

(3) *The school as moral educator*: This section examines the role of the school as moral educator. Education, if it is to be authentic, involves a moral dimension. The moral life is taught by the school that has character and virtue. The school has the twofold task of morally teaching and teaching morality. In other words, the school community and its physical environment models how one should live. In this sense, it teaches without end. This form of teaching is complemented by another form of moral education, namely, teaching morality or ethics. Ethics involves the systematic reflection on the moral and ethical questions and issues of our time. This way of educating has an end in view. Both forms of teaching are indispensable in order to fulfill the essential moral dimension of education.

The final section of Chapter 5 discusses how the school as educator, teacher and moral educator educates towards adulthood. School has an important role to play in enabling children and adolescents to embark on the journey towards integral adulthood. It can help them to develop into mature people who are capable of working towards integration and reconciliation with the world. Moreover, in an age of increasing secularisation, school has a responsibility to educate the rising generation towards a greater understanding and appreciation of religion throughout their entire lives. This includes the ability to converse about religious matters in the language of intelligent public opinion.

The sixth chapter, 'The Parish as Religious Educator', presents the parish as educator. In this regard, it discusses how the parish or congregation can execute both aims of religious education by teaching religion and teaching to be religious.

(1) *The parish as educator*: This theme explores what it means for the parish to educate religiously. The parish educates, first and foremost, by being a community. In order to illustrate this form of education, it is necessary to explain what a community is, what its characteristics are and how it educates by modelling a way of life. In ecclesiastical language, community educates by being a form of *koinonia*. Community is experienced in the three types of parishes found in our contemporary world – the super parish, the intermediary parish and the mini parish. While the mini parish is small enough to form a single community, the larger parishes may comprise a group of small communities. These are usually known as basic Christian communities. Within the community setting, the parish educates by modelling a way of life through the manner in which it engages in liturgy and service. This occurs through preaching and catechesis and models a way of life to parish members and to the world.

(2) *The parish as teacher*: In making the distinction between the verb *to teach* and the verb *to educate*, this section illustrates how numerous people, who are not called teachers, cooperate in the educational enterprise. In the parish community, people of all ages and walks of life participate together and teach, often unintentionally, in ways that are primarily non-verbal. The parish community is responsible for teaching religion as well as teaching people to be religious. In terms of the latter, the homiletic and therapeutic languages of teaching find a home in the parish setting. Storytelling, preaching and, occasionally, lecturing can be appropriate teaching languages for the parish community. Since the parish community, like all human communities, experiences brokenness, the therapeutic set of teaching languages are also used. Moreover, religious faith has an intellectual dimension and an adult member of the community should be able to articulate his or her faith at the level of common understanding. In this regard, the teaching of religion in the parish setting is explored. Teaching to be religious already takes place within the parish, but the pertinent question concerns whether the teaching of religion as an academic subject can also be made available. Does the present structure of parish life have the freedom to engage in good conversation about religion?

(3) *The parish as moral educator*: This section illustrates how the parish or congregation educates morally. The parish educates morally by being a parish and the moral life is taught by the parish that has character and virtue. The congregation educates morally by design and by example. The design best suited to educating morally in the parish is that of community and the manner in which it morally educates is by modelling a life of service. In this regard, the ecclesiastical term of *diakonia* (service) is explored. Three specific ways in which the parish educates morally by design and by modelling are also examined – teaching morally, teaching morality and teaching morality

(ethics) in the classroom of the church. With these in mind, we take note of Kevin Nichols who writes that 'morality is not a sub-department of religion', but 'has its own way of working as a language has its grammar and syntax.'[1]

This final section of Chapter 6 examines the important role play by the parish or congregation as educator, teacher and moral educator in educating towards adulthood.

In order to explore the manner in which the parish engages in this task, it is necessary to examine the ideal of adulthood towards which the congregation educates. In addition, the conflict between adult growth and Church authority is noted, together with the various ways in which the parish can educate towards adulthood. In this regard, all the parish's educational forms are directed toward psychological, social and religious maturity.

The book concludes with an epilogue born out of the insights and learnings of the previous six chapters. It synthesises and brings together the various threads that make up the tapestry of religious education and in so doing outlines principles for a new approach to religious education for the third millennium.

I wish to thank many people who supported me in the writing of this book. The Sisters of St Louis enabled me to follow my dream and pursue doctoral studies at Fordham University, New York. Dr Kieran Scott, my mentor, introduced me to Gabriel Moran and accompanied me through the writing of my dissertation on which this book is based. Drs Gerald M. Cattaro and Barbara L. Jackson generously gave of their time, reading my dissertation and making recommendations. Gabriel Moran met with me on several occasions and furnished me with challenging and thought-provoking information. The Diocese of Ferns enabled me to put flesh on and implement much of the findings of this book. Dr Oliver Brennan, my colleague and friend, opened up his house to me, provided me with the space to write this book and gave me a listening ear as

I teased out many of its thoughts. A special thank-you to my father, Gabriel Cunnane, who painstakingly proof-read my manuscript. Fr John-Paul Sheridan and Martin Brennan also read the manuscript and provided helpful recommendations. Finally, I am so grateful to my parents, Gabriel and Mary, and my siblings Enda, Gaye and Aidan for their continual support and encouragement.

1   K. Nichols, *Refracting the Light*. (Dublin: Veritas, 1997), p. 97.

Chapter I

A BABEL OF LANGUAGES

It is my conviction that religious education is one of the most important issues facing our world today. It is also my belief that religious education is of little importance to society as a whole and that it does not achieve supreme acknowledgment in the Christian Churches. This is partly due to the narrow understanding of the meaning and purpose of religious education. If religious education is perceived as an activity that engages in proselytising and indoctrination, then society is right in regarding this action as insignificant. However, if religious education is understood as that which pertains to the centre of human life and is recognised as contributing to the quality of our being in the world, then it is, undoubtedly, an indispensable endeavour. Such an understanding recognises that religious education is an activity that educates religiously throughout the life of the human person. In order to explore this more fully, it is helpful to examine the current reality of religious education with a view to re-imagining a fuller meaning of this task at this crucial point in our history.

The Current Reality
Religious education in many parts of the world is narrowly understood as that which takes place within either the school or

parish setting. Predominantly directed to people between the ages of five and eighteen years, religious education is taught with the title varying from *catechetics*, to *religion*, to *religious knowledge*, to *religious studies*, to *religious instruction*, to *Christian doctrine*, to *Christian education*, to *religious education*.[1] In Roman Catholic circles, the content for younger children concerns their introduction to the basic truths and doctrines of their faith and includes their preparation for the sacraments of Penance, Reconciliation, Eucharist and Confirmation. This is catechesis in its classical form. The curriculum content for older children and adolescents frequently involves a deeper exploration of the truths and doctrines learned earlier in life, as well as issues pertaining to adolescent growth and development. In some countries, religious education at post-primary or high-school level includes the study of religion as an exam subject.

Confining religious education to the school or parish setting and directing it solely at those aged between five and eighteen years has highlighted many problems for those involved as well as for concerned others. While many efforts have been made to establish links between the key forms of life that educate, for example, family, school and parish, the educational contribution of some of these forms tends to be diminished or excluded when religious education is confined to a single setting. In Ireland, for example, school is the context for religious education and the schoolteacher is the religious educator. This results in an unwarranted burden being placed on the schoolteacher and excludes others from the conversation. In an age of growing secularisation depicted by a 'decline both in church attendance and in the overall significance of religion for individuals and for society' the burden for schoolteachers increases.[2]

Problems arise when the catechetical dimension of religious education is confined to the school setting. The faith formation of young people takes place outside of the faith community and sacramental preparation is automatically embraced when one reaches a certain class or grade. Family, school and parish no longer engage in the same conversation nor speak the same language. The result is that the religious education learned in school frequently clashes with the lived experience of the young person outside of the school setting.

This story of religious education throughout the world points to a number of problems inherent in its implementation. The first concerns the absence of a field that can be accurately named religious education. A dearth of research and theoretical scholarship results in religious education being regarded as a duty or obligation rather than a field in which to be engaged. With little or no recognition of the adult population, religious education is addressed, almost exclusively, to school-aged children and, even at that, is considered to be an appendage to *real* education. Not considered to be of primary importance, many schools and churches allocate a minimum of resources to religious education and nobody seems to be concerned.

A second problem inherent in religious education pertains to the *babel of languages* used to describe what takes place. Although they possess varying meanings and differing sets of assumptions, the words *catechetics, religion, religious knowledge, religious studies, religious instruction, Christian doctrine, Christian education* and *religious education* are judged to be synonymous and are used interchangeably both in literature and in conversation. As a result, different people mean different things when using the term *religious education.* Attaining consensus regarding the use of terms is a necessary and essential prerequisite for any discipline or field of study, particularly that of religious education.

The *babel of languages* and interchangeability of terms has led to confusion and a crisis of identity regarding the activity of religious education and the role of religious educators. Confusion of identity leads to confusion of purpose. The third problem, therefore, concerns the purpose of religious education. What is the purpose of religious education? The variety of interpretations of the term *religious education* has resulted in a multiplicity of understandings of the purpose or aim of religious education. This was highlighted in Ireland with the introduction of Religious Education as an exam subject. Questions arose concerning the meaning of religious education. Does it concern the academic study of religion or the catechetical formation of a person? This situation points to a fourth concern, namely, the absence of a coherent theory of religious education, a theory that would outline the philosophy, assumptions, and foundational principles of religious education and, at the same time, serve to dissipate the confusion of purpose and crisis of identity that abounds.

The story related above points to the reality of religious education in many areas of the world, as many well-renowned international religious educators will attest. For example, religious educators such as Gabriel Moran and Kieran Scott continually seek to address these issues and contribute to their clarification. For over thirty years, Gabriel Moran has noted the absence of a field of religious education, has sought to break open the meaning of words in order to bring about linguistic clarity and has called for an adequate theory of religious education.[3] Kieran Scott acknowledges similar concerns.[4] Calling for order in the area of religious education, Scott contends that the field of religious education is not clearly defined. No consensus has been reached with regard to key terms. The purpose of religious education is unclear and more attention must be given to the theory of religious education.

The Linguistic Debate
In order to grapple with the four above-mentioned problems of religious education, it is necessary to pay attention to terms in an attempt to unravel and unearth the history, set of assumptions, and world-views embedded in the various expressions used to describe religious education. Therein lie the clues to understanding religious education in its broadest sense.

Indeed, Gabriel Moran believes that the meaning of the term *religious education* determines whether religious education is a thing of the past or 'an idea whose time has not yet arrived.'[5] He proposes that religious education be explored by means of two directions.[6] One direction would be to describe the way in which religious education is and has been used, i.e. the *term* of religious education. The second direction would involve an exploration of the *meaning* of religious education. By that is meant what could and should be included in the meaning of religious education. Both directions require exploration.

Beginning with the first direction and concentrating on the origins of the term religious education, the aim is to unravel the history and set of assumptions contained in this term as well as in the terms with which it is interchanged. In order to do this, it is helpful to examine the positions of leading scholars in the field, thereby taking them into our conversation. Only when this has been accomplished can the fullest idea of religious education be explored.

Thomas H. Groome

In approaching the topic of religious education, Thomas H. Groome begins with an analysis of the meaning of education in order to name this activity. He then proceeds to deal with the notion of religion which he weds to education. It is within this context that he names the activity of *religious education* as 'a deliberate attending to the transcendent dimension of life by which a conscious relationship to an ultimate ground of being is promoted and enabled to come to expression.'[7] However, he regards this activity as incomplete and goes on to name religious education, undertaken by and from within the Christian community as *Christian religious education* which he defines as

> a political activity with pilgrims in time that deliberately and intentionally attends with them to the activity of God in our present, to the Story of the Christian faith

community, and to the Vision of God's Kingdom, the seeds of which are already among us.[8]

Of particular importance in this statement is Christian religious education's participation in 'the political nature of education in general.'[9] Education, by its nature, is a political activity since it influences how people live in, and shape the future of, society.

In relation to *catechesis*, Groome writes that coming from the Greek verb *katechein*, meaning *to resound, to echo*, or *to hand down*, catechesis, throughout history, is understood as oral instruction. In this regard, he disagrees with Berard Marthaler who understands catechesis as 'a process whereby individuals are initiated and socialized in the church community.'[10] Neither is he happy with John Westerhoff III who sees it as the entire process involved in becoming a Christian. Naming these two understandings as 'Christian socialization or enculturation', Groome argues that such redefinitions are so far removed from the word's etymological, scriptural, and historical roots that they are hardly accurate and certainly not useful.[11] Furthermore, there is a major disadvantage in redefining catechesis in such a broad manner because 'it fails to name and thus severs the Christian educational enterprise from its commonality with education and religious education.'[12] If this occurs, then where does one begin to engage in catechetical activity? According to Groome, it is more accurate and more helpful that our understanding of the word catechesis is consistent with its etymological, scriptural and historical meaning, that of 're-echoing or retelling the story of Christian faith.'[13] Catechesis, therefore, is a specific instructional activity situated within Christian religious education.

Mary C. Boys

Acknowledging that the field of religious education is relatively young (dating from 1903), Mary C. Boys recognises that its practice is considerably ancient. In recent years this has led to many questions being posed regarding the understanding and intentionality of religious education, as well as what it means to educate religiously. According to Boys, religious education identifies the classic expression that 'weds classic liberal theology and progressivist educational thought.'[14] This leads her to define *religious education* as 'the making accessible of the traditions of the religious community and the making manifest of the intrinsic linkage between traditions and transformation.'[15]

In discussing the term *Christian education*, Boys notes that the term began as a theological critique of religious education by calling into question the relation of religion and culture. Criticising the advocates of religious education for the attention they gave to world religions, psychology and the social sciences, the proponents of Christian education regarded theology as central, allowing it to control Christian education. According to their perspective, the task of Christian education was to form faithful disciples of Jesus Christ, with the focus being on an ecclesial holiness. Interestingly, such an understanding of Christian education has undergone contemporary modifications. For example, C. Ellis Nelson advocates the use of the social sciences and replacing dialectical theology with other theological perspectives.[16] Randolph Crump Miller believes that equal voice must be given to theology and education in Christian education.[17] While these modifications may be commendable, their introduction has served to reveal the lack of clarity surrounding the nature and purpose of Christian education.

Boys goes on to equate Catholic education with catechetics, stating that Catholic education was the most inclusive term in existence until directly after Vatican II, when the term *catechetics* became more dominant. The genesis of catechetics lies in the kerygmatic movement, a renewal movement that originated in Europe in the 1930s, whose aim was to return to biblical and liturgical roots. Recognising the unity of scripture and tradition, the Catholic Church undertook scripture study, thereby grounding catechetics in the bible, and recognising its link with the liturgical life. As a result, new understandings emerged and the task of catechetics was perceived as deepening conversion 'so that people can better discern God's ways in the social sphere and, thus, participate in the churches prophetic mission.'[18] Such an understanding of catechetics does not differ greatly from Boys' own definition of religious education. This is a clear example of the *babel of languages* that is in existence.

Kieran Scott

Kieran Scott understands the activity of religious education as the synthesis of religion and education. Recognising that *religion* and *education* infiltrate most areas of our lives, religious education is a 'particular and pervasive need confronting our society'.[19] It is seen 'as a test of the maturity of our culture, the health of our institutions and the quality of our lives together.'[20] Aware that contemporary society understands religious education in a restrictive manner by confining it to the context of Church and ecclesial language, Scott sets out to free the assumptions, claims and perceptions lying behind the variety of terms.

Beginning with catechetics, Scott traces the history of the term from early Christian times to the present, painting a panoramic picture of how our understanding of the term has changed. Moving into the contemporary catechetical scene in the United States, Scott turns to the *National Catechetical Directory* of the United States, entitled *Sharing the Light of Faith*, for a comprehensive description of the meaning of catechesis. According to this document, the term *catechesis* involves the entire process of 'maturing in the faith' and 'refers to efforts which help individuals and communities acquire and deepen Christian faith and identity through initiation rites, instruction, and formation of conscience.'[21] While *Sharing the Light of Faith* contains rich catechetical insights, Scott's reservations with it focus on the three major issues of language, Church pattern and education. 'The linguistic world of catechetics', he writes, 'is decisively ecclesiastical and narrow in context.'[22] With regard to Church pattern, Scott critiques its structures as bureaucratic and hierarchical and calls for their reform. In relation to education, he criticises the Church's refusal to be identified with this activity, contending that 'when religion is placed in an educational context, it can make a decisively positive contribution to personal development and the quality of public life.'[23]

Taking the issue of language a step further and analysing the *National Catholic Directory's* use of the terms *catechesis* and *religious education*, Scott outlines the editors' struggle with both these terms, and notes their movement from using the terms interchangeably in the initial stages, to omitting the term *religious education* in the final draft. This resulted in the term *religious education* being 'absorbed into catechesis', an action which served to determine the nature and focus of the directory.[24]

In an effort to illustrate the differing and vitally important tasks of *catechesis* and *religious education*, Scott analyses the world of catechesis and outlines its constitutive elements. Representing the Roman Catholic tradition, the main concern of catechesis is 'to maintain the tradition, pass on the heritage, and solidify one's religious identity.'[25] This lifelong process takes place through 'socialisation, enculturation, and evangelisation....', and, is the task of the whole Christian community.[26] Acknowledging the strengths of this ecclesiastical viewpoint, Scott also notes its limitations, arguing that 'catechesis does not and cannot contain the wide range of concerns and contexts which the term religious education denotes.'[27] Religious education is more than socialising people into the Catholic Church. Differing from catechesis in terms of context, content and curriculum, Scott points to the educational mission of religious education whose task is 'to insert critical openness into church ministry and to bring educational critique to current church forms.'[28] This leads him to conclude that the terms *catechesis* and *religious education* cannot be used interchangeably. 'The former', he writes, 'is limited and restricted to an ecclesial semantic world, whereas the latter has the ability to house the full range of religious and educational questions and concerns emerging in contemporary culture.'[29]

Gabriel Moran

Like Scott, Gabriel Moran acknowledges the lack of consensus regarding the use of the term *religious education* and points to the extraordinary difficulties that abound in attempting to define its meaning. He states that *religious education*, a term that came into vogue in the twentieth century, can be narrowly understood as that which some people do in some places, or it may be more broadly employed to include 'the practices that govern people's lives in every time and every place.'[30] Stating that the schools of England and Wales use the term *religious education* in the clearest way, Moran notes that in these countries 'the term does transcend particular religious parties and has taken on a legally established meaning.'[31] In these countries a clear definition of the term can be traced to 1944 when the British Government rendered religious education compulsory in state-supported schools. Here the meaning of religious education was religious instruction that was to be executed in accordance with 'an approved syllabus and a daily assembly for worship.'[32] Since 1960, this meaning has been modified due to two major developments, namely 'increasing doubt about the value of compulsory worship in state schools and a greater pluralism of religion in many English schools.'[33] This has resulted in religious education becoming almost synonymous with religious instruction, not in the sense of being confined to knowledge of the Bible or a single religious tradition, but with an openness to understanding many of the world religions. In England today, the term religious education refers to 'the name of a subject taught in state schools.'[34] Such a reference, Moran contends, stands in stark contrast to the way in which the term is understood and employed in the United States of America.

In order to reveal the historical assumptions and understandings of religious education, Moran outlines a history of the term as it unfolded in the USA. The term *religious education* came into being in that country with the founding of the Religious Education Association, (REA). The REA was founded in 1903 when four hundred people, mainly Protestants of liberal denominations, came together to search for an educational approach to religion. They articulated a three-fold purpose for the new movement:

- To inspire the educational forces of our country with the religious ideal;
- to inspire the religious forces of our country with the educational ideal;
- and to keep before the public mind the idea of Religious Education and the sense of its need and value.[35]

Hoping to improve upon the educational ideal offered by the Sunday school and to approach religion in public and Church schools in a more scholarly fashion, the aim of the REA was to create an academic field of religious education, as well as a religious education profession.

The underlying foundations of the REA comprised liberal theology, the social gospel and the progressive educational movement. These three currents of thought contributed to the success of the REA during the 1920s. Up to this point theology had been influenced by the strong patriarchal religion of the nineteenth century in which God saved the human person from sin and damnation. This gave way to a more liberal understanding of religion in which people were in charge of their own religious lives. Inspiration for moral living was gleaned from the bible. Language remained biblical, with the powerful image of the *Kingdom of God* being retained, an image that for some become synonymous with self-realisation. The chief value of religion was deemed to be *social:* that is, it provided the rules, inspirations and insights for people living together in a democratic society.

The liberal education movement aimed to follow the challenge of John Dewey that religion be 'public, generally known, and tested in ordinary ways.'[36] As a result, education in the school setting adopted some of the ideas and roles of religion. The eighteenth century's trust in reason reached fruition in the nineteenth century's trust in science. Science became key in education literature, as well as such phrases as *social, democratic, child-centred life situations*. This was an exciting time. Change in the world was accelerating, psychology was revealing insights previously unknown and George Albert Coe was questioning the primary purpose of Christian education. Was it 'to hand on a religion or to create a new world'?[37]

Circumstances changed, however. The experiences of the Depression and the two World Wars resulted in a pessimism concerning the human person. In addition, the influence of European neo-orthodox theology by theologians such as Karl Barth and Emil Brunner began to question the origins of liberal religious education. It was deemed that doctrinal substance had eroded within the Protestant Church. Karl Barth retaliated with his neo-orthodoxy and returned the *Word of God* to the centre of theology, a movement which paralysed the Religious Education movement and one from which it never recovered in its original form.

In 1940, the publication of Harrison S. Elliott's book, *Can Religious Education be Christian?*, marked a critical moment. Elliott challenged neo-orthodox theology, accusing it of being authoritarian and interfering with people's free choice in relation to religious matters. His thesis was to resist what neo-orthodoxy had to offer and return to the promulgations of liberal theology. The following year, H. Shelton Smith, in *Faith and Nurture*, addressed the same predicament, but with a different outcome. His concern was 'shall Protestant nurture realign its theological foundations with the newer currents of Christian thought or shall it resist those currents and merely affirm its faith in traditional liberalism?'[38] Smith's option for the former alternative marked the beginning of a new era. A new breed of educationalists emerged and they replaced the term *religious education* with the title *Christian education*. The outcome was that the Protestant Church regained control of its own education, thereby shifting the direction of religious education and, thus, the hope of creating a new profession died. The failure to admit this resulted in *religious education* and *Christian education* being used interchangeably in Protestant circles.

Since the 1960s, the term *religious education* has experienced some revival in the United States and is associated with the teaching of children outside Catholic schools. While the term is more frequently used by Catholics than by other denominations, no consensus of meaning for the term exists, even within the Catholic Church.

By way of summary then, it can be seen that the term *religious education* is used in two distinctive ways. Religious education refers to religious instruction that takes place in the classroom and it also refers to a Church sponsoring activity of religious socialisation. The future life of the term, therefore, depends on two major factors – the inclusion of non-schooling elements of education into the understanding and meaning of education (a factor which would include the very young, as well as the adult population) and the development of 'a systematic and comparative study of religious practice.'[39]

Exploring the meaning of Religious Education

Having examined the *term* of religious education, it is now possible to turn to the second direction in which religious education can be explored, that is, the *meaning* of religious education. Gabriel Moran, in his attempt to explore the fullest meaning of religious education, indicates a need for two languages of religious education – an ecclesiastical language and an educational language. While both languages have their strengths and weaknesses, it is important to note their complementarity. Ecclesiastical language needs the language of education to prevent its being threatened by parochialism. Conversely, the language of education requires the concreteness of religious organisation, but it must not be reduced solely to Church language. Such a reduction serves to perpetuate the current problem of equating religious education with catechetics in the Catholic tradition and Christian education with religious education in Protestant circles. It must be recognised that the term *religious education* is broader in meaning than catechetics or Christian education.

Ecclesiastical language comprises the two components of theology and catechetics/Christian education, with theology governing their content. The appropriateness of the word *theology* has been questioned, however, and it has been suggested that this word may not be necessary or even helpful when speaking about a Christian position.[40] The role of theology is to provide one model among many as a means to understanding religion. Theology's failure to understand itself in this light has resulted in its control of catechetical language; a factor that renders dialogue impossible and serves to limit the effectiveness of the work carried out by catechists and Christian educators. Rather, dialogue within the Churches can be facilitated by placing the study of religion into an educational context instead of in an ecclesiastical setting.[41]

An educational context seems a more appropriate context for religious education than the ecclesiastical. While similarities exist between the school's control of education and the Church's control of religion, it is important to distinguish between education and school. Education has been described as 'the systematic planning of experience for growth in human understanding.'[42] This depiction of education recognises the possibility of religious issues surfacing in all aspects of life. In this regard, religion is referred to as that which 'pertains to the origin, destiny or deepest meaning of our world and finds expression in social gestures.'[43] Existing as 'personal attitude, communal symbol and bodily behaviour, the religious is something out of the ordinary that calls the ordinary into question.'[44]

Recognising the tension that exists between the words *religion* and *education*, particularly as one gets closer to a fuller understanding of education, it is important to recognise that both words need each other in order to become fully effective. Education needs religion lest its institutions become obsessed with bringing the ordinary under control. Similarly, in an effort to break out of the ordinary and refuse any form of restraint, religion needs the influence of education's guidance and temporal forms.[45]

While it is possible for all education to have religious significance, it is essential to include three areas of education in religion where religion is recognised and honoured. These comprise: (a) the study of a specific religion from within; (b) the study of religion from a position of some distance; (c) the practice of a religious life.[46]

Taking each in turn, the study of a religion *from within* invites one to turn away from introversion or defensiveness in relation to one's own religion and to perfect one's vision, viewing the world through the eyes of another. Such an activity implies an appreciation of things for their own uniqueness. The task of religious institutions is to appreciate everything in this way.

The study of religion *from a distance* is also crucial as a component of a full religious education. This element of religious education means observing one's own religion in relation to other religious and nonreligious options. Educational institutions provide the best forum for this form of religious education.

The third element of a full religious education concerns the practice of a religious life, a practice that can be briefly summarised by prayer and social action. Because of the private and intimate nature of many of these practices, (for example, contemplation, the sacraments, and social justice), this aspect of religious education cannot be studied or taught. Rather, this meaning of religious education can be tested in its ability to retain what is most valuable from the past, while at the same time opening new possibilities for the future. The challenge of religious education now is 'to help us speak and live the truth we know while also removing the intolerance which is embedded in our language.'[47]

These three areas of education draw attention to two approaches to religious education that ought to be avoided: proselytising and indoctrinating on the one hand, and simply understanding explanations of religion on the other. The former terms have negative connotations, while the latter is too removed from the religious life. What is needed is the development of the religious life of humankind. In this regard, religious education needs to be understood as that which concerns 'the religious life of the human race and with bringing people within the influence of that life.'[48] There are two distinct, yet complementary, ways to foster this development. These comprise (1) the understanding of religion (which pertains to what happens in the classroom and in academic institutions), and (2) formation in being religious, that is, the catechetical. A fuller exploration of these two aims of religious education can be found in a later chapter.

Four Qualities of Emerging Meaning

In order to extend the conversation, Gabriel Moran points to four essential qualities that must be included in our fullest meaning of religious education. First, religious education should be *international*, that is, take into account the variety of national meanings of the term. While academic religious education in most countries is in some way related to national governments and while many religions have a trans-national character, an international dialogue or discussion is difficult because of the lack of a common language. There is no universal meaning of religious education and the term *religious education* is translated differently in different languages. Scholars in other disciplines who meet internationally may have a common text (albeit with some variations) as a basis for discussion, whereas an agreed general area for religious educators is more nebulous. Perhaps Ireland, a nation that has been significantly influenced by the UK and the USA, is a good example of a country which, instead of being a satellite to the international dialogue, may be instrumental in developing the fullest meaning of religious education. Indeed, the Irish situation provides an opportunity to integrate the UK meaning (schooling in religion) with the US meaning (formation in religion). Both meanings are needed for a comprehensive theory of religious education.

The second aspect or quality of conversation needed for religious education is *inter-religious* dialogue, a quality that is inherent to religious education itself. The need for this aspect of religious education has arisen with the growth of religious pluralism. Indeed, education in interreligious dialogue is essential for international cooperation and for the future security of humankind. This is highlighted by Eleanor Nesbitt who focuses principally on the Sikh tradition while making reference to studies from the Hindu and Christian experience. Contending that agreed boundaries separating faith traditions are becoming increasingly anachronistic, she argues for greater openness in religious education in order to expose the dynamics of religious and cultural evolution.[49] It is interesting to note here that the term *inter-religious* provides a broader forum than the narrower title *interfaith* because *inter-religious* connotes the visible and tangible aspects of faith that can be dealt with educationally. Religious pluralism is not just about multiplicity. It is about affirming the importance of each religion, but only in relation to all of the others. In other words, pluralism and relativism are understood positively. This, however, requires authentic education within each religious group and between groups. If religious pluralism has been the factor that led to religious education, then religious education is the basis for sustaining religious pluralism. Religious education in this context may then be understood as having two aims: (1) a heightened awareness and appreciation of one's own religious life and (2) a deeper understanding and appreciation of the religion of others.

When speaking of religious education, Gabriel Moran prefers to use the image of learning a second language. Our first language is our faith/religious language, the language we acquire and absorb from our religious/ecclesiastical tradition, and one that pertains to the ultimate in life. Religious education as a second language begins to emerge when our first religious language is compared with an entirely different one. Using the analogy of *lingua franca,* religious education can be understood as the attempt to bring many religious languages into one conversation. The importance of such a framework is essential in the promotion of understanding, tolerance and world peace. Such a conversation would result in a better understanding of one's first religious language, as well as a deeper appreciation of the religious languages of other traditions.

Third, religious education should be *intergenerational.* Aware that many people understand education as that which happens to children, religious education may lead the way in promoting a lifelong education. The concept of intergenerational education is an important reminder that people are being taught continually by those who are older than them as well as by those who are younger. Indeed, 'the most dramatic embodiment of intergenerational education is the conversation between the old a few years from death and the young a few years from birth.'[50] Religious education can contribute to education generally by encouraging the relation of the very young and the very old. The very young and the mature adult often have a profound religious sense and this can be salutary for those going through the hustle and bustle of the middle years.

Finally, religious education should be *inter-institutional.* Life-long education goes hand in hand with life-wide education. Similar to life-long, intergenerational education, life-wide education correlates particularly well with religious education. In order to be effective, education must engage the major institutions of society. Cooperation between religious bodies (Christian, Jewish, Muslim, Hindu, Buddhist) and public institutions is extremely important and the pitfalls of total identification and total opposition must be avoided. Rather, their roles are to be regarded as complementary. How does this work out in practice? The primary responsibility of the State is to provide the resources necessary for education and religious education, whereas the vocation of the churches is to model a religious way of life.

Conclusion

In advocating a wider conversation for religious education, we are invited into a deeper journey, a journey into the quest for richer meaning. An easier route would be the path of definitions, the concern with defining terms. However, the 'road less travelled', the road that resists the definition of terms, invites the traveller to break open words in order to allow the deeper levels of meaning to emerge. Only when this happens can important changes take place. It is to this that we now turn.

Chapter 2

SETTING THE FRAMEWORK FOR THE CONVERSATION

In order to explore the deepest meaning of religious education, I will place before you three major themes that are in need of clarification – *The Meaning and Forms of Education*, *The Meaning and Forms of Teaching* and *Moral Education and Educating Morally*. These themes are the signposts for our conversation and invite us to explore the 'road less travelled'.

1. The Meaning and Forms of Education

Current educational language narrowly perceives school as *the* form of education. Central to this misunderstanding is the use of the terms *formal* and *informal* education. These terms came into being in an attempt to differentiate between school and education. The result is that the term *formal education* is used synonymously with and controlled by school, while the phrase *informal education* has been presented as an umbrella term assigned to the rest of education. The word *education*, however, connotes form. This renders the phrase *formal education* redundant and reveals that *informal* or *non-formal* education is a contradiction in terms. The world of education does not consist of one single form but, rather, comprises a multiplicity of forms. In this respect, the language of formal and informal education serves to limit conversation and hinders a genuine exploration of the other educational forms in existence.

Ultimately, the unreflected use of these phrases threatens the health of school and other forms of education.

The perception of school as the *only* form of education is further exacerbated by the denial of the religious question present in the meaning of education. There is an inaccurate presumption that religious education is a branch of theology and is, therefore, the responsibility of churches and synagogues. This belief results in a resistance to its inclusion in the modern understanding of education. Conversely, there are people working in the religious area who, while not wishing to be separated from education, are opposed to being confined totally to an academic environment. Religious education is a part of education and any attempt to explore the meaning of religious education must begin by questioning the meaning of education itself. As Gabriel Moran puts it, the 'religious problem is buried deeply in the meaning of education.'[1] What is lacking is a basic language in which to ask educational questions.

Gabriel Moran argues that education is an interplay of life forms.[2] Acknowledging that there is no single genuine meaning of education, he states that the meaning of the word is found in its use. The way in which the word *education* is used can be traced historically through its etymology and through the ways in which changes in its meaning have occurred throughout the centuries. It can also be traced geographically by examining the manner in which various groups understand its meaning today. Therefore, in order to reclaim, reform and restate the meaning of the term *education*, it is necessary to examine two key issues: 1) the etymology and history of the word, and 2) the people rendered voiceless through their exclusion from its current meaning. Because education is identified with the schooling of the young, the absence of infants, very young children, and the elderly from educational literature is noteworthy. The voiceless include women who, in the past, were restricted from the establishments that control the *meaning* of education. Both these omissions have led to a deficiency in the meaning of the term *education*.

History of the Word

The use of historical studies in paving the way towards an understanding of the constitutive elements of education is particularly useful. In one historical example education pertained to the nurturing and rearing of children. Each generation had a limited period of time in which to pass on valuable knowledge to the next generation, thereby depicting education as highly directive. The difficulty with this understanding is that it tends to be authoritarian and, thereby raises profound questions concerning human freedom.

In pre-modern times, education had no single form and was not directed towards a clearly specified age group. Education in this era took place through 'traditional family patterns, religious doctrines and rituals, and apprenticeship for one's station in life.'[3] Educational reform, however, became necessary with the introduction of the modern sciences and its accompanying analysis of religion. Religion had failed to give people what they were looking for. School became the new place of worship, and education, in this setting, was to provide the key to success.

The nineteenth century saw protests in relation to the school being regarded as the only form of education. The 'adult education' movement, for example, considered the equation of education with the schooling of the young as totally inadequate. They envisioned 'twentieth-century educational centres where people of any age would learn from a wide range of experiences.'[4] One of the reasons why this dream has not been realised is due to the badly deficient educational language that, for example, qualifies the word education with the adjectives *adult* and *continuing*. What this has done is to place adult education as an appendage to the (real) education that is directed toward children.

In order to illustrate the institutional pattern of education, it is helpful to turn to Bernard Bailyn's treatment of the history of education.[5] In his research, Bailyn questioned whether, throughout history, all the educating was done by the school.

His conclusion was that, while schools did have a part to play in education, that part was not necessarily as large as people had heretofore surmised. He reinstates the elements of family and church, elements previously dismissed by John Dewey as being inadequate educational possibilities. This leads him to describe a configuration of four educational institutions – family, school, church and apprenticeship – all of which helped in the transmission of the culture to young people in the colonial period of the seventeenth century.

Gabriel Moran affirms Bailyn's four-part description of education as providing 'a definite pattern of language that has historical credibility.'[6] However, he criticises him for adding the elements of Church, family and apprenticeship to the schooling form of education. Such an understanding is flawed because, in hijacking the meaning of education, school has ceased to be a form of education. Rather, it has become an institution within which education is situated. The interaction of educational forms cannot take place when other forms are added to the school. The task, then, is 'to name the main forms that shape human existence by a *lifelong* and *lifewide* interaction.'[7]

Donal Oliver and Fred Newmann's reference to a threefold pattern of education: community seminar, schooling and laboratory, is also noteworthy.[8] However, their educational language, and that of Bailyn, fails to provide the clarity and concreteness necessary for a contemporary understanding of education. 'Further distinctions within the main elements of education' that would better describe the 'interactions that *are* education' are needed.[9] The community seminar category of Oliver and Newmann is, perhaps, the most exciting and may provide one of the clues to understanding education, that is, what it means to be community and the relationship between family and community. Education may be perceived as the shaping and reshaping of this fragile relationship between family and community. Failure to include this in the meaning of education is an illustration that the point has been missed. It is this relationship between family and community that prompted Moran to name other patterns of life that educate. Ultimately, his educational pattern comprises four forms: family, schooling, work and leisure. These forms will be explored in more detail at a later stage. Now, however, it is necessary to turn to the second key issue that has contributed to the current meaning of education – the voices excluded from the meaning of education.

Voices Excluded from the Meaning of Education

In order to recapture the true meaning of the word *education*, it is essential to pay attention to the voices that have been excluded from its current meaning. For example, in the past, women were excluded from the establishments that directed the *meaning* of education. The result was that women were not educated in the place called education. In addition, the operative meaning of education did not include their experiences – experiences that differed radically from the experiences of men. The result was a fundamental deficiency in the meaning of education. Consequently, women developed alternative forms and aspects of education.

Another group excluded from the meaning of education include those rendered silent because of age. When education is associated with school-going children, and 'adult education' categorises people into adults and children, other groups such as infants, very young children, and the elderly are ignored. This deficiency has resulted in *education* being generally understood as 'the affair of young and middle-aged adults exercising power in the lives of older children and young people who are soon to join the ranks of these adults.'[10]

Forms of Education

While acknowledging that people in recent centuries had a broader conceptualisation of education than we have today, this is not to advocate transposing their meaning of education to our present age. Instead, we need to invite people to assist in the birthing of a more imaginative meaning of education commensurate with the needs of the twenty-first century. In this respect, Gabriel Moran calls for a lifelong educational pattern that begins with the identification of 'those forms of life in which people are taught how to live.'[11] This is not to invent something new, but rather to recover what was in existence in the past and what continues to be a reality in the present, albeit peripheral.

Ideally, education should be about the interplay of various institutions. This requires a change of human activity on the part of the educator, as well as a change in the way people relate to other people and to the non-human world. Such an understanding of education is not concerned with schoolteachers facing schoolchildren, but rather with describing the interplay of institutions that comprise education.

Gabriel Moran presents a model of education that distinguishes between two forms of education – schooling and laboratory. Schooling is a 'form in which people intentionally use space, time, materials, and people to acquire knowledge and skills.'[12] This form of education is not confined to people between five and eighteen years, but spans a person's life from birth to death. There are two great moments contained within this form of education. These comprise the individual's experience from within existing concerns, prejudices and premises, as well as his or her aptitude to distance oneself as a thinker. 'Schooling', according to Moran, 'is a moment for the emphasis of distancing though never to the complete exclusion of experience from within.'[13]

Three components make up Moran's laboratory or non-schooling part of education: family/community, work, and retreat. With regard to family, it can be noted that little change has taken place in the family unit over the centuries and it is not likely to change much in the future. The *family* is a compelling form of education. Three points here are noteworthy: the family form of education teaches, parents and children are in a reciprocal teaching relationship, and the homiletic, therapeutic and academic teaching languages are found in family life.

As with family/community, the importance of *work* to an individual's sense of identity and self-worth is significant. Work and education are in a reciprocal relationship, with work being educational and education often providing training for work. Since work-related issues are frequently the contemporary adult's point of entry into education, a change is required in the way one perceives work and life. This means recognising the role of work in the lives of children, women and the elderly.

Retreat means quiet reflection and can be understood as being a 'counterpoint to the rest of a person's education.'[14] Central to this position is an understanding of retreat that expresses a profound 'human experience of completeness' and is expressed in a multiplicity of ways, 'ranging from utter stillness to exuberant play.'[15] Retreat or leisure education has two aspects: retreat/leisure itself educates and, at the same time, it is possible to educate for retreat/leisure. A great test of education lies in the presence of a retreat that is both at the centre of one's life and at the centre of a community.

The issues of work and leisure are particularly relevant for religious education. The paradoxes surrounding these elements are concerned with the realm of religion and, therefore, it is important that they be included in a definition of religious education. At the same time, religious education plays a role in the interpretation of work/leisure. In distinguishing between education *to* work and education *by* work, as well as education *to* and *by* leisure, it is also important to make two further distinctions: between job and work and between leisure as free time and leisure as contemplation. Anchored in religious history and part of our contemporary language, these two distinctions differentiate between the ordinary and the greater-than-ordinary aspects of life. Job and free time are part of the ordinariness of life, whereas work and contemplation are understood to be invitations to something greater. According to Moran, 'these distinctions are religious if one means by religious the attempt to affirm what is greater than the ordinary.'[16] 'A religiously educational approach', he continues, 'is to affirm what is more than ordinary while not denying the ordinary or undercutting its value.'[17] This insight prompts the examination of the meaning of work and leisure in greater detail.

Recognising that work is not synonymous with paid employment, the reader is invited to name and appreciate the forms of work portrayed by children, young people, the elderly and women. The word *work*, therefore, needs to be inclusive of these groups of people and attention paid to the work in which they engage. Such a task will transform the work-world as it opens up to all sectors of the population. For example, the work contribution of those who have retired from the labour force involves sharing the richness of their wisdom and experience. People in this category can contribute greatly to the understanding of work. Similarly, the work of people, the majority of whom are women involved in childcare and housework provides an invaluable contribution to society and, when taken seriously, changes the whole meaning and understanding of work.

In understanding leisure as contemplation, we are talking about an attitude of being centred, being whole, being at peace. A contemplative person is not one who is withdrawn or detached from the world, but rather is one who resides at its very centre. With this understanding, whether they are on or off the job, people are invited to seek out quiet places and quiet times in order to cultivate an attitude of leisure and contemplation.

In conclusion then, religious education is that which affirms and ameliorates a person's work and, at the same time, brings him or her to the realisation of being a co-creator with God in transforming the world. In a similar fashion, religious education is concerned that people experience free time in such a way that their lives 'move toward the still point at the centre of the universe.'[18]

The Universal Values in the Life-Forms of Education

Understanding education as an interplay of the key life forms that educate necessitates an outlook on human life that is constantly open and developing. Moreover, it requires a lifelong educational curriculum, one that is open to a developmental idea of education. These life forms, however, are only educational to the extent that they embody universal values. The educational forms of family, schooling, work and leisure are partial embodiments of community, knowledge, work and wisdom. These value-laden terms represent a universal good and present themselves as images for the whole of education. In this respect, education may be described as 'a movement toward community or work or knowledge or wisdom.'[19] This is an educational pattern that can be shaped and reshaped. In attempting to embody its universal value, each educational form requires the presence of the other three values, albeit a background presence. For example, family will succeed in being a place of community only if, secondarily, it is a place of work, wisdom and knowledge. Similarly, when schooling, job and leisure are the main forms of learning, the other three values are present in the background. It is important to note here that only one of these forms is prominent at a certain stage in our lives. Family, for example, is the main form of education for infants and young children. As the child gets older, family retreats to the background and schooling becomes the main form of education. From young adulthood through mid-life, work is the centre through which education takes place. Leisure is more prominent for the elderly.

By way of summary, then, education can be understood as 'the interaction of forms of life with end (meaning) and without end (termination).'[20] Acknowledging the existence of innumerable social forms pertaining to human life, Moran delineates four lifelong and lifewide forms – family, schooling, work and leisure. Family is the first form of education experienced by a child. When the child gets older, he or she receives instruction in a classroom setting. As they mature, people are expected to participate in the workforce in order that life may be nurtured and enhanced. Finally, once people reach retirement, they are invited to participate in leisure activity. Therefore, the four forms of family, school, work and leisure may be seen as a lifelong progression, and as providing the basis for a theory of education.

A more beneficial educational theory requires the interaction of these life forms at every stage of a person's life. At any given age, any one of the four forms can come to the centre, while the others remain at the periphery. For example, when a child goes to school, schooling comes to the centre and familial education moves to the side. Family does not disappear, but works in partnership with the classroom. Similarly, when work and leisure come to the fore, people continue to be taught by what they have learned from infancy.

Each of the four social forms 'is a partial embodiment of some ultimate value that can stand in for the purpose of education.'[21] For example, the values of community, knowledge, work and wisdom are partially embodied in the forms of family, schooling, work and leisure respectively. The family educates to the degree that it is truly community, school educates to the degree that it truly provides knowledge, work educates to the degree that it is truly work and leisure educates to the degree that it truly brings wisdom. These social forms, together with their embodied values, provide the curriculum of education and, through their interaction, illustrate that education is always 'with end and without end.'[22]

Having considered the meaning and forms of education, it is now helpful to consider the meaning and forms of teaching.

2. Meaning and Forms of Teaching

What is the meaning of the verb *to teach*? The answer to this question lies in a comprehensive exploration of the meaning of teaching. There are numerous books written about the teaching activity, but the majority of them fail to question the meaning of *to teach*. Those which do focus attention on the subject consider only one form of teaching – school-teaching, with the assumption that 'teaching is an explanation from the front of the classroom'.[23] Such a presumption serves to undermine the importance and essence of teaching. This form lacks the context needed to describe an effective – and moral – approach to teaching, even in this particular setting. Gabriel Moran explains why:

> when teaching is equated with classroom instruction in a school, what disappears are not only most kinds of teaching but also the language, imagery and techniques for improving classroom instruction itself. The one kind of teaching that is thought to be defensible is left morally indefensible.[24]

Questioning why teaching is so narrowly perceived, Moran is aware of people's uneasiness with the idea of teaching and suggests that this feeling of un-ease has led to 'a deep suspicion that teaching is an immoral activity.'[25] Such a conjecture results from a legacy inherited from the eighteenth century when teaching was understood as an activity in which an adult exerted power over a child.

In offering an alternative assumption to the relationship between teaching and learning, Moran begins by saying that people learn because they are taught. Human beings are taught 'by other human beings, by the religious tradition, by the marvels of creation, and ultimately by the divine teacher.'[26] Noting that the founders of most religious traditions were honoured with the title *teacher*, he draws attention to the fact that contemporary theories of education cast aspersions on teaching because of a bias against religion. This is a result of modern European writers rebelling against Christianity, an action that caused them to abandon teaching as well. Consequently, the meaning of the term *to teach* has been reduced to 'a rationalistic core devoid of religious meaning'.[27] This understanding is still in vogue today.

The current rationalistic perception of teaching restricts the work potential of teachers in religious education. In order for religious educators to effectively teach a way of living religiously, a variety of settings is required, only *one* of which is the classroom. Therefore, 'any successful revolution in education will have to include a re-appropriation of the many forms of teaching.'[28] The challenge for religious educators, then, is to 'retrieve the best of their own traditions and bring that wisdom into conversation with modern writing on education.'[29]

The Meaning of Teaching: Teaching and Education

In distinguishing between the verb *to teach* and the verb *to educate*, it is important to note that many people, who do not hold the title *teacher*, are involved in education. Teaching, on the other hand, involves engaging in an activity that is directed towards another. This act contains a certain degree of intentionality. Here the teacher is directly concerned with a person's learning and takes steps to ensure such an outcome. The teaching act occurs 'along a spectrum which runs between (1) the doing of a skill which requires bodily training; (2) the demonstration of a pattern of language.'[30] The first supplies the primary tool for deliberating upon teaching. The second affords a language that enables people to control and understand their lives in a more advantageous way.

The entry point into the examination of teaching begins with bodily actions. The human learner is constantly concerned with the body, with the result that 'the elements of teaching bodily skills are present in all teaching.'[31] Teaching involves the verbal and non-verbal. Therefore, it is important that the teacher relates words and body in such a way that the words used are experienced in bodily feeling. In this regard, it is necessary for a teacher to be in touch with the bodily genesis of language, as well as the social controls that language embodies.

A great teacher shows how to name, describe and state what disturbs, challenges and beckons the learner in order that bodiliness in language is demonstrated. This language is not the invention of the teacher, but rather emerges from the wealth of 'human meaning embedded in ordinary speech.'[32] The teacher's task lies in providing a means of processing information in a way that invites the emergence of the total person. Only when this occurs can the predicament of coercion in teaching be by-passed.

By way of summary, it can be seen that education concerns the whole of life, but 'teaching most appropriately occurs at the point of penetrating inhuman control and at the peak of expressing human freedom.'[33]

The Meaning of the Verb 'To Teach'

It can be said that contemporary educational theory has diluted teaching to the provision of information through giving reasons and explanations. A more comprehensive understanding of teaching is one that regards teaching as an activity in which every human person and some non-humans engage. The human person learns almost everything he or she knows by being taught, thereby, illustrating that teaching is 'one of the most important and regular acts we perform in life.'[34] Teaching means *showing someone how to do something*. It is an activity that may or may not embrace reasons, explanations or information. In its most complete expression, *to teach* is 'to show someone how to live', a process which almost always contains a moral dimension.[35] In this regard, it can be said that teaching also includes a religious aspect because showing someone how to live eventually includes showing someone how to die.

This comprehensive meaning of the verb *to teach* leads to the next crucial step: liberating it from the fetters of its most rationalistic form. In this regard, Moran calls for an examination of 'the unconscious behavior and indirect intention of the teacher', as well as a study of the 'non-person world, including nonhuman nature and human institutions.'[36] Confining an examination of teaching to that which takes place in the interpersonal relationship between teacher and student serves to limit the world of teaching from which and within which the individual human teacher is trying to work. 'The ultimate subject of 'to show someone how to do something'', he notes, 'is the universe of living and nonliving things.'[37]

Concerned with the human/nonhuman interplay in the teaching activity, Moran focuses on some basic teaching forms that take place unintentionally, unconsciously and, for the most part, non-verbally. Acknowledging Michael Oakeshott's examples of the sea, the book, and the self as suggested modes of teaching, he recognises the teaching possibilities contained in all forces of nature, whether they are as great as the sea or as minute as the snowflake.[38] However, he is surprised by Oakeshott's rejection of *the book* as teacher and writes that 'the book is the closest we can get to most of our human teachers, living and dead.'[39] While the self is always present in human learning, claiming it as the only source of learning is to deny the people, books, and forces of nature that direct and substantiate learning.

In exploring human and nonhuman teachers, it is necessary to pay attention to our next of kin – the animal. Renewed interest in the study of animals has provided insight into their ability to learn. The fact that animals learn seems clear, but the rhetorical question is 'Are they taught?' If teaching is understood as showing how, then animals are indeed taught when they undergo training of any kind. This is most evident when a human being engages in the teaching of an animal. But, what is the case when the animal is trained by another animal? Does a mother bird teach her fledgling to fly or train her offspring in the art of obtaining food? In these circumstances what is taught is deemed to be extremely restricted.

Notwithstanding these limitations, human beings can learn significant lessons from animals. Take, for example, the manner in which animals engage in ritual when dealing with inter-species conflict.[40] Another example concerns the fact that we humans are also animals, a factor most evident in the teaching of very young children. Moreover, the animal constituent of teaching takes place in the physical continuity of the relationship between teaching and learning. This aspect is clearly depicted in the life-preserving practices perpetuated by animals without the use of explanations. Such an observation points to the fact that infants must be included in any theory of human teaching.

The type of teaching that takes place in the human community has marked human qualities. Occurring without any degree of intentionality, this teaching, for the most part, is non-verbal, and can be examined in two ways – by *example* and by *tradition*. Teaching by example is most effective when teachers *are* examples rather than when they *give* examples. In being examples, the lives of the most effective teachers are illustrations of how to live and how to die. This unveils one of the greatest paradoxes concerning human life – it is only possible for some of the most important teaching to occur when *intention* is absent. The essence of teaching, therefore, does not lie with intention.

Teaching by tradition represents another aspect of unintentional and nonverbal teaching, and takes place through the aural, the oral, and the tactile. This is most evident in the relationship of a mother with her child, who through the way she handles the infant, transmits the human experiences of love, care and security. 'All teaching', Moran writes, 'is showing how', and all teaching commences with 'hands on'.[41] Therefore, it is no coincidence that the etymology of the word 'tradition' is *to hand on*. Tradition, in this sense, is not what is handed on but, rather, is the handing on.

The Forms of Teaching

a) Teaching by Design

An exploration of human teaching can begin by investigating the way in which we teach by design. Connoting a twofold meaning, the term *design* 'attempts to capture both the express interest of the human teacher and the material limits of what can be taught.'[42] To teach by design, therefore, can pertain to a deliberate human objective or it can relate to the design used by the teacher. The specific act of showing someone how to do something unavoidably entails design. This design changes in accordance with the student's activity and the environment. For example, the family, school and parish teach by design. They teach unintentionally through the way in which they are designed, that is whether they are authoritarian in style or whether they are designed in a community-like fashion. They also teach intentionally through the design employed in showing someone how to do something.

The relationship between teaching and learning may be described as a single process, as two sides of the same coin. This premise, however, is in conflict with several philosophers, including Wittgenstein and Aquinas, and with modern educational theorists whose assumption is that a gap does exist between these two activities. Declaring a continuity between *teach* and *learn*, Moran believes that 'there is a gap that can never be eliminated between the *intention* of the (human) teacher, translated into a set of gestures, and a result called learning on the part of another.'[43] This gap between intention and result becomes more apparent as the teaching design moves from mostly physical action to predominately human speech. Consequently, it is necessary to 'find out what *is* teaching in a particular situation and then direct one's attention to redesigning these forces.'[44] For example, in order to teach a human being operating in a physical environment, the existing design linking the person's activity and the environment must be changed. The language used in this case is one of instruction. However, human beings have mastered the use of language in such a way as to expand their facility for learning. This leads Moran to outline other forms of language operative in teaching. He does this with a word of warning:

… the underlying metaphor of design should not be forgotten: to teach is to show someone how to do something, how to choreograph a human body's movement. No matter how abstruse and theoretical teaching becomes, it never severs its roots from the metaphor of design.[45]

b) Teaching with the end in view

In discussing the act of teaching, it is necessary to differentiate between three groups or families of languages. The effects of the first two families are in opposition, despite the fact that both deduce meaning from their physical environment. The third family infers meaning from reflecting back on the other two. *Storytelling, lecturing* and *preaching* comprise the first family of languages in teaching with an end in view. Here, language is employed 'to show someone how to get to an end that is known and can be chosen'.[46] Taking place within the community, the intention of this set of languages is to influence people to behave on the principles of community beliefs. The role of the teacher is very important and is regarded as a temporary assignment in order that a mutuality of persons is preserved. The teacher must rely on a style that is in touch with the 'memory, faithfulness, hopes and conviction' of the community.[47] This must be done in such a way that the underlying beliefs of the community are recaptured and placed in a new configuration. The task of the teacher 'is to link the past with this end in the future so that the energies of the present are unleashed.'[48]

With little room for critical thinking, this first family of languages is 'concerned with speech in relation to bodiliness.'[49] The first embodiment of this family is teaching by *storytelling*. There are numerous forms in which storytelling exist. These range from a parent telling fairytales to a child, to the great stories of history, to the community's own story told and retold through the repetition of ritual. Teaching within storytelling occurs in the telling, with the result that little or no explanation is required.

The second language in the first family of languages is the *lecture*, a term connoting reading. Indeed, 'lecturing is a highly ritualised act in which a person addresses community; the end that the lecture has in view is some rational conception of humanity.'[50] The lecture, therefore, aims to change the actions of the listener.

With regard to *preaching*, very little difference exists between the lecture and the sermon, except that lectures are read, while sermons are spoken. Closely associated with the church, the sermon reflects upon a text expressive of the community's beliefs with the aim of directing the listener toward involvement in acts of peace and justice. Making use of intimate language, the test for any preacher is to move the hearts of the community, while ensuring that outsiders are not insulted or offended. Although they may never admit it, other groups frequently involved in preaching include politicians and journalists, as well as the television advertisements that demand the viewer to act by purchasing their product. In this regard, Moran writes:

> The relentless television advertisements are perhaps a symptom of what happens in a culture when storytelling, lecturing and political preaching are ineffective. The culture becomes addicted to preaching of the worst kind while thinking it has escaped the preaching of sermons.[51]

By way of summary, the teaching languages of storytelling, lecturing and preaching presuppose a specific set of circumstances – a group of people open to the power of language. The way in which the teacher engages language is as important as the spoken word, whether the teaching occurs through story, lecture or sermon. To teach with this first set of languages, then, is to incite people to action by 'appealing to their understanding of the beliefs of a particular community that is representative of the whole human community.'[52]

c) Teaching to remove obstacles

Teaching, in recent centuries, has been closely associated with the first set of languages described above. In other words, to teach has been understood as *to explain*. The explanatory form of teaching, however, requires the assistance of another set of languages – languages to remove obstacles. These are called *therapeutic* set of languages. At first glance, these languages may appear to have no connection with the art of teaching, but these are the languages that calm, soothe and heal. In the right context, they are the languages necessary to show someone how to live and how to die. Therapy is central to human life and, therefore, should be regarded as pivotal to teaching.

The therapeutic set of languages presupposes a fragmented community in which the individual is searching for his or her identity. Human communities, by their very nature, are flawed groups and members often feel disconnected. The use of language serves to heal the fragmented person in order to open up the possibility of choices. Included in this family of languages are *praise, thanks, confession, and mourning*. These languages can be paired as follows in order to draw attention to the reciprocal nature of the therapeutic: praise/condemn, welcome/thank, confess/forgive, mourn/comfort.'[53] These languages of ritual are crucial teachings in that they show us how to live and how to die in a world that does not always make sense. They have the potential to heal the split within us by providing an initial experience of the meaning of salvation, i.e. 'the health, wholeness, and holiness that religions promise.'[54] A deeper examination of these paired languages will reveal the essence of their teaching activity.

Praise/Condemn: This first pair of languages, praise and condemn, is linked with the homiletic family of languages in that storytellers, lecturers and preachers frequently praise or condemn. Indeed, both praise and condemn begin with an outlook toward the cosmos, and are concerned with both the natural environment and human achievement. The verb *to praise* is used to portray the language called forth by awe and wonder. It is, 'the special response of the human being to being human within a universe of surprise, beauty and invitation.'[55]

The word *praise* is paired with the verb *to condemn* and acknowledges that the relationship is one of opposites. Whatever destroys that which is praiseworthy is worthy of condemnation. While good teachers do not condemn, it is important to note that anger, in relation to intolerable situations, is justifiable. What is recommended is that this anger would lead to vigorous action aimed at alleviating destructive elements in our world.

Welcome/Thank: This pair of therapeutic languages can be described as 'reciprocal and interlocking expressions' in the sense that 'welcome is a kind of thanking and thanking is a form of welcome.'[56] Welcome/thank resembles praise and condemn in relation to their concern with the universe as a whole, but they differ by virtue of their presence in interpersonal relations. Teaching by welcome/thank begins with an open receptivity to all of creation and all of life. It is an attitude that overflows into expressions of welcome toward other human beings. The thanking correlative of welcome also pertains to the universe as a whole and includes individual people. 'To the extent that someone feels welcome in the universe', Moran writes, 'the recipient of miraculous gifts, then expressions of gratitude are called forth.'[57]

Confess/Forgive: The confess/forgive pair of languages is important when the flow of human life is interrupted. The weakness and vulnerability of our human nature necessitates the ritual of confession in order to restore the split that has occurred within the human person and within the life of the community. Recognising the promises inherent in the teaching languages of stories, lectures, and sermons, other teaching languages are only effective when healing has been restored. This highlights the importance of forgiveness, and recognises that confession can only be experienced as healing and restorative in relation to forgiveness, an act which results in the recreation of the world.

Mourn/Comfort: The final life experience of all people – dying – is the concern of the last pair of languages in the therapeutic family. Here the basic meaning of teaching is to show someone how to live and how to die. The avoidance of death means the avoidance of teaching. The languages of mourning and comforting, therefore, must be included in all languages of teaching. Furthermore, the language of mourning is crucial to all other teaching languages. This is because the emotions concerning grief and loss need to be given expression if people are to focus on the joy and sadness in their own lives, as well as in the lives of others. Similar to the other therapeutic languages, the language of mourning necessitates ritual, ritual that will lead us to experience the teaching language of comfort. This understanding also recognises the need for comfort in all the minor hurts and crises that characterise the minor deaths we experience in life.

d) Teaching the conversation

The two contrasting families of teaching languages discussed above remind us that the first family was concerned with the end view of the community and the languages necessary to direct the individual toward that goal. The fragmented community, on the other hand, together with the languages that bring healing, were the focus of the second family. Now a third family is introduced, one that presupposes and reflects back on the other two. The focus in this family of languages concerns the form of teaching that is 'speech about speech', where 'language is examined in relation to itself'.[58] This entails questioning the meaning of the beliefs held by the first two families of languages, as well as the meaning of their relationship with each other. Put more concretely, it concerns 'changes of metaphor, an examination of the language of the language of teaching.'[59]

One way in which this can be done is through the differentiation between truth and meaning, a distinction that gives license to a playfulness with language. 'Meaning', Moran writes, 'invites the play of imagination and the testing out of alternatives.'[60] This facility for playfulness is the hallmark of maturity. Indeed, it is impossible to comprehend the third family of teaching languages unless the teacher possesses an ironic sense of humour. The languages of *dramatic performance, dialectical discussion* and *academic criticism* are included in the third family of teaching languages.

Dramatic Performance: Dramatic performance is one of the ways in which language can be played with in the life of an adult. Plays can be representative of the first two families of languages in that some plays have the ability to convey a message, while others are concerned with the various troubles of life. The play is also concerned with teaching the conversation and is, thereby, invited into the third family of languages. In this situation, the play transcends the teaching languages of the first two families and reflects on language itself. An example of this is evident in some of Shakespeare's plays where a play is often found within a play. A contemporary example is the movie, *Shakespeare in Love*. In a similar fashion, plays of the twentieth century, rather than tell a story, are often a reflection on storytelling and other forms of speech. An illustration of this can be seen in some of the comedy routines played by Laurel and Hardy and the Marx Brothers where their continual misunderstanding of each other draws attention to the ambiguities of language.

Dialectical Discussion: Acknowledging that dialectical discussion may just be another name for dialogue, the word *dialectical* is used in an attempt to imply 'a more reflective use of language and a concerted effort to find the meaning of the words in the dialogue.'[61] Dialectical discussion emanates through conversation and through reading and calls for the otherness of the text to be respected. In other words, dialectical moments occur when someone is able to walk in the shoes of another and experience the world from that viewpoint. While the idea of dialectical discussion may, in the opinion of many, be traced back to Socrates, it did find its place as the mode of argument in the Middle Ages when the Fathers of the Church were seen to have had conflicting views on many issues. In the twentieth century, the term *dialectical* came into prominence with Marxism where it was used to highlight the conflicts of class differences.

Academic Criticism: Dialectical discussion paves the way for academic criticism, the last language in the third family of languages. Incorporating all the previous languages, academic criticism has the potential to be the most powerful of the teaching languages. In acknowledging the other two families of languages, academic criticism is provided with materials on which to work in the form of stories, lectures and sermons from the first family of languages, and is equipped to achieve the distance it needs from the second family. In addition, academic criticism shares in the questioning of language found in dialectical discussion. Academic criticism differs from dialectical discussion, however, in understanding the student as participant rather than spectator. In this situation, the student's own words become the main point of reference as well as the focus of criticism.

Since community is the locus of academic criticism, the absence of community quickly sours criticism. Indeed, 'the practice of academic criticism presupposes knowledge, discipline and care of one's colleagues', and should, therefore, be the focal point of classroom instruction.[62] In other words, a classroom does not function as a classroom unless academic criticism is present. Therefore, it is important to have academic dialogue between teacher and students, conscious that ironic questioning is the sign of academic criticism.

By way of summary, it can be seen from the above discussion that Gabriel Moran has examined language from the point of view of being 'separated from bodiliness', with the teacher's task being 'to choreograph ... a movement of language.'[63] In this respect, the first two families of teaching languages 'are concerned with speech that is separated from bodiliness'.[64] They have immediate contact with the body in terms of inviting the human person on a journey that leads to an integrated and healthy individual and communal experience of life.

The third family does not have immediate contact with the body. Rather, it has contact with other languages and is concerned with meaning, intellectual understanding and with questioning every form of life. This takes place within human conversation, with the aim of inviting forth better forms of life. 'This form of teaching', Moran concludes, 'can never replace the other forms, but with their help it can transform the world.'[65] Teaching, then, is not simply classroom activity executed by a schoolteacher, but that human and non-human potential of showing someone how to live and how to die.

3. Moral Education and Educating Morally

The issue of morality or ethics comes to the fore in any attempt to delineate a satisfactory meaning of religious education.[66] Indeed, the relationship between morality and religion has enjoyed a prominent position in the history of Western civilisation. The 1960s, however, ushered in a new stream of writing on morality, ethics and values, a wave that continued through the 1970s. Benefiting from the twentieth-century studies on child development, this new body of writing appears to be contaminated with the perennial problem of separating morality and religion. While such a distinction is desirable in order to appreciate the essence of both, their reunion is important for the healthy functioning of society. Any attempt to dissociate morality and religion results in two expositions of unease: (1) People's lives are affected by religion, even unintentionally, with the result that religious issues continually filter back into the conversation; (2) the positive potentialities contained in religious attitudes, experience, ritual and language are not taken into account.

The Genesis of Moral Education

Gabriel Moran examines the twentieth century's effort to deal with morality under the rubric of *moral education*.[67] Moral education, as a single term, came to birth at the beginning of the twentieth century. Prior to this, the words *moral* and *education* had a separate existence. While these words were no strangers to each other, the predominant thought, at that time, considered the phrase *moral education* to be redundant. Education was perceived as a moral activity from the days of the Greek philosophers. However, as the nineteenth century drew to a close, the advancement of science, together with the declivity of religion, resulted in education being considered amoral. People were faced with a choice. One could remedy the situation with the presence of *moral education*, or one could 'rethink the moral character of all education.'[68]

The origins of the moral education movement can be traced to the early phase of modernity. The hope of the seventeenth and eighteenth centuries was that science and religion would become compatible. Scholars, it was hoped, would be influenced by science, while the *modus operandi* of the remaining population would be through the myths of religion. Under this arrangement, education was perceived as a science. As education developed along with science, religion began to withdraw. The result was that the foundation of morality in the lives of the majority was excluded from, and even hostile to, education.

The beginning of the twentieth century witnessed a strong basis for morality, together with a total distrust of religion. The time was ripe for the launching of a stringent moral education. With the timely appearance of Emile Durkheim's *Moral Education*, the term *moral education* came into being. Describing what was happening, he wrote:

> We decided to give our children in our state-supported schools a purely secular moral education. It is essential to understand that this means an education that is not

derived from revealed religion, but that rests exclusively on ideas, sentiments and practices accountable to reason only – in short, a purely rationalistic education.[69]

Durkheim's book, however, reveals some reservations regarding an education that is purely rational. According to him, the moral life is lived in community and, therefore, is not based on reason alone. The family, therefore, is an inappropriate place for a purely rationalistic education, whereas 'the task of the school in the moral development of the child can and should be of the greatest importance.'[70] To teach morality within the school, 'is neither to preach nor indoctrinate; it is to explain.'[71] Such a flight from preaching and indoctrination leads Durkheim to reduce the activity of teaching to the giving of explanations. This, however, had 'the unfortunate effect of giving over most of moral education to processes other than teaching.'[72]

Theories of Moral Development
Studies concerning the child's capacity for moral reasoning centre on the works of Jean Piaget. Interested in how children come to make abstract judgments, he focuses on those judgments regarding the ordering of society and names them moral judgments. In this respect, the word *moral*, for Piaget, is almost synonymous with *social/affective.*

Piaget defines morality as follows: 'All morality consists in a system of rules, and the essence of all morality is to be sought for in the respect which the individual acquires for these rules.'[73] In keeping with its Kantian influence, this narrow definition of morality perceives moral development as the individual's capacity to reason about a system of rules. Here, Piaget's uncomplicated scheme of moral development moves from rules being understood as external to their being perceived as necessary for the good of each person. Rather than referring to two stages of morality, Piaget speaks of *two moralities* through which the child slowly moves between the ages of six to twelve years approximately. The first morality, called *heteronomous*, reveals that rules are regarded by children as external, sacred and unchangeable. Nothing that adults do can alter this perception. A second morality is named *autonomous*. This begins by paralleling the first, then conflicting with it, and finally replacing it. With the emergence of the second morality, the child begins to appreciate the advantage and purpose of rules and realises that they are neither untouchable nor external. The intention behind their creation and recreation by the human community is to enable the healthy functioning of the social order. Now the child begins to comprehend the ethic of justice as the balance of mutual respect, a movement greatly enhanced by the interplay that takes place among children.

Piaget's understanding of morality points to a direction beyond these two moralities when the individual sees that the world is not equal and grapples with how to live in a world that is not just. His suggestion is that issues of intimacy, care, compassion and love now take precedence. This further stage of development may be regarded as a deepening of the second morality.[74]

Lawrence Kohlberg, through the inspiration of Piaget's thinking on morality, proposed his own scheme in the 1950s. Concerned with education, he was dissatisfied with the placement of moral education between two inadequate positions – indoctrination and values clarification. This led him to propose two stages with regard to moral rules: '(1) an egocentric stage with arbitrary rules externally imposed; (2) a socialised stage with necessary human rules to maintain a social order'.[75] He then adds a further stage of moral development – the *postconventional*. His belief is that full moral development entails living by principles of justice that are disconnected from context and intention and, thus, implies that social living is nothing more than the following of conventions. Moral development for Kohlberg, therefore, is concerned with the movement from doing in order to please, to doing for the purpose of law and order. Such a movement is limited by virtue of its non-universality.

Kohlberg's theory has proved to be very popular, not least because of his claim to offer moral education completely divorced from religion. This does not sit easily with Moran who criticises him for not investigating 'the possibility that religion and morality could have a mutually beneficial relation.'[76] Moran argues that both religion and morality make claims towards universality. Religion needs morality lest it become irrational and destructive and morality needs religion in order to shape vision, provide stories and direct desires. Kohlberg's belief that religion has no significant effect on morality stands in conflict with the creeds of the Jewish and Christian peoples. For them, morality and religion are intimately related, a factor that has affected history down through the centuries. In Moran's eyes 'Kohlberg's total separation of morality and religion obscures what is present in people's lives.'[77]

The discussion thus far operates from the assumption that the word *morality* can be easily defined. Morality, for Piaget, comprised rules and the individual's respect for rules. For Kohlberg, morality entailed compliance to a single rule of justice perceived as equality. Morality, above all, involved *reasonableness.*

Acknowledging the contributions of Piaget and Kohlberg, Moran proposes an alternative way to image, conceptualise and articulate morality. He refers to 'virtue/care/character/community as the interlocking categories of an alternative approach to moral development.'[78] He begins by examining the most interesting contribution made by Carol Gilligan when she criticised Kohlberg's work as being sexually biased. Gilligan attempts to illustrate that a theory of human development is not possible until the relation between the sexes ceases to interfere with the procurement of reliable data.[79] In studies using Kohlberg's scale, she found that women ranked lower than men in studies of moral reasoning. Her suspicion was that women might be speaking in a different language. Studying women who were contemplating abortion, her empirical data revealed two stages of moral development commensurate with the lives of her subjects. These comprise (1) 'a stage that was egocentric and irresponsible', with the woman's only concern being for survival, and (2) 'a stage of trying to live by society's rules' in an attempt to recognise and care for the other.[80] Gilligan also discovered a stage of moral reasoning beyond these two stages, one that stands in stark contrast to Kohlberg's postconventional stage. She names this stage *trans-moral* and writes that it occurs with the reintegration of one's concern for survival into the responsibility and care for others.[81] Moran notes that a radical reconstruction of morality is brought about by this stage with the focus being on a care and compassion inclusive of oneself and the other.[82]

Gilligan understands Kohlberg's morality as being a morality of rights, whereas she sees her own as a morality of responsibility. While the idea of responsibility is commonly used in the fields of ethics and morality, Moran points out that Kohlberg's theory 'does have a kind of responsibility to the rights of others and to the principle of justice.'[83] In this regard, he believes that Gilligan parts company with Kohlberg 'in her answers to the questions of to whom, with what, and for what purpose are we responsible.'[84] The supposition in Gilligan's theory is that we are responsible to others, with our moral selves, for the purpose of caring for people and nature.

Moran's Response
Moran believes that a theory of moral development devoid of religious imagery and language is absolutely inadequate. In this regard, he affirms Gilligan's exploration of an ethic of care, stating that it gets close to the religious. The role of religion in moral development is crucial in that it provides a community narrative of what people we belong to, as well as furnishing us

with exemplars of a moral/religious life from which we can learn. 'Religion', Moran writes, 'gives a sense of adventure to the moral enterprise and thereby sustains the necessary discipline for the moral life.'[85] This can be manifested through the moral notions of virtue/care/character/community, an ethic communicated largely through inspiration and imitation.

Moran's belief is that *virtue* including *care* will lead us back to character in *community*.'[86] While Kohlberg tends to deride the word virtue, an alternative to his judgment and principle may be procured through reflection on the virtues and on the virtuous person. The etymology of the word virtue lies in the Latin translation of a Greek word denoting *strength* or *excellence*. An integration of strengths is said to be the hallmark of the virtuous person. According to Plato, Aristotle and Aquinas, people become virtuous through their participation in the life, story and vision of the moral community.

Character results from response to the social and physical environment in which one lives. Moral development is dependent upon other people and other things and, therefore, the role of the community is essential in the moral development of a person. According to Moran,

> One of the marks of a community is the story its people hold in common, a story expressed in symbols, codes of behavior, styles of humour, modes of dress and address, ways of sharing sorrow and the like.[87]

The inclusion of the above ethic in a theory of moral development is particularly beneficial to the formation of the young child. Rather than being pre-moral, the child of five or six years of age can be profoundly moral and aware of the forces of good and evil. Indeed, infancy and childhood provide opportunities for some of the most important aspects of moral development and moral education to take place. This occurs through the care received by the child as well as through his or her experience of games, stories, image formation and language. Moral development, therefore, begins from the first moments of life and continues until the individual takes his or her last breath.

The Concept of Development

Noting the dearth of written material on the concept of development itself, Moran observes its presence in almost every field of study today.[88] The word *development* is suggestive of a change for the better and, because of this, is used to understand both individual and cultural change. It is in this regard that the issue of moral development is central to development. To progress to a better stage implies knowledge of what is good and bad, of what is right and wrong.

The term *development* is most frequently used by psychologists and economists. Moral development is considered as belonging to psychological development, especially since Piaget's publication of *The Moral Judgment of the Child*. Moran's belief, however, is that moral development should be associated with all the fields using the word *development*. 'In ways that are not measurable', he writes, 'moral development has some connection to physical, social, political, religious, and other kinds of development.'[89]

Moran claims that the modern western world is attached to the image of a ladder to the sky, a ladder that invites people to climb upward in search of success and the good life. Development theory, he believes, is a dramatic illustration of such a ladder upward. According to this theory, an individual proceeds through a series of hierarchical stages by climbing the ladder one rung at a time. The writings of Kohlberg have taught us to imagine moral progress in this way. For many people, moral development and moral education involve climbing the six steps in Kohlberg's system to the highest stage of moral development.

Reflecting on this question for many years, Moran notes that the problem does not only lie with the image of ladder, but with imagery itself. 'Discussions of human morality', he contends, 'require a language that breaks free from the imagery of visible, acquirable objects and instead emphasises lively, earthy, communal, and politically powerful metaphors.'[90] In this regard, he dismisses the image of ladder or staircase for development theory, preferring Maria Harris's figuration of steps in a dance. Patrick Devitt suggests the images of 'symphony' and 'ballet'.[91] Development has to be a movement towards harmony, integrity and endless fulfillment. The movement of moral development needs the imagery of a 'constant circling back on oneself and the recapitulating of life at a deeper level.'[92]

Ages/Stages of Moral Development: It is commonplace to speak of stages when referring to development or moral development. Piaget, for example, delineates three stages in the moral development of a child, while Kohlberg outlines six. Progress is charted along a straight line, depicting the stages as 'hierarchical, invariant, and sequential.'[93] While this is true for moral reasoning, moral development is a much more complex affair, and, therefore, cannot be measured. 'It involves a continuing recapitulation of the past in service of an ever-precarious synthesis in the present.'[94]

This description of moral development makes the distinction between age and stage. Each age of life is reached by staying alive and each stage of moral development is reached by responding to what life presents at every age. Every person, therefore, gets to and through every stage, but in different degrees. Education closes the gap between age and stage. Through a reshaping of life forms, its moral quest is to ensure that each age is better. If development is to be a lifelong affair, then education, obviously, has to be lifelong too. Whatever constitutes good education constitutes moral education. Conversely, 'moral education extends to whatever truly deserves the name education.'[95] Moral education, therefore, begins from the first moments of life and 'continues throughout life in the symbolic articulation of physical, communal activity.'[96]

Morality and Education

Moran states that the narrow understanding of moral education currently in existence stems from two defects in its development earlier this century: (1) the insistence that morality be divorced from religion; and (2) the supposition that education is synonymous with schooling.[97] Both Durkheim and Piaget, through their anti-religious attitude and their application of ethics to the education of children, have contributed to this myopic understanding. The result is that the meaning of *moral* and the meaning of *education* in moral education is altogether too narrow. By way of response, Moran invites dialogue to take place between education and morality, thereby setting up a new classification of writing – *educational morality*.

Educational language: A distinction between schooling and education is necessary if the unendurable burden of moral education is not to fall on the schoolteacher. Such a distinction is not intended to belittle schools and their teachers, but seeks to free their work through a broader understanding. While some may feel that the distinction between schooling and education is apparent, there is no educational language in existence that is inclusive of the very young and the very old. The real problem with education is the assumption that it is a product available in school. Education, as we have seen, is broader than school or schooling and includes all the life forms that educate. An educational morality, therefore, must do likewise. This means including the religious form of life that has been excluded from the contemporary meaning of moral education.

Moral language: In turning to moral language, one is not leaving the educational realm behind. Rather, the word *education* contains a moral value. When one understands *morality* and *education* as essentially the same process, then 'morality, or at least moral maturing is the reshaping of life's forms with end and without end'.[98] As a result, Moran suggests three stages in the process of maturing morally, depicting them as follows.

The first stage of *uneducated morality* recognises that each person is born with a morality. As the young child is immersed in the discipline and ways of a community, he or she imbibes a sense of right and wrong. This factor forms the basis of all later morality. Morality, in this first stage, is *uneducated* as the customs, codes and rituals absorbed by the child 'have not been exposed to a reshaping toward greater meaning.'[99]

Ethical thinking dominates the second stage of the moral life. Here morality is reflected upon through the use of analytical reason with the view to forming a dependable system of principles or rules. The individual now wishes to make his or her own decisions regarding the right thing to do. The provision of an ethics course is particularly beneficial at this stage.

Educational morality marks the third stage of the moral life. While there is no exact age specification for this stage, it presupposes the maturation of the preceding two stages. At this stage, the rituals and symbols acquired in childhood reappear, having been refined and translated once again by rational intellect. Moral decisions at this stage can be an enjoyable experience.

Teaching Morally, Teaching Morality
Two of the basic questions in moral education concern whether morality can be taught and whether a system of moral development exists. Contemporary answers have been *no* to the former and *yes* to the latter. Morality, it is deemed, cannot be taught since development is a natural occurrence. The paradox lies, however, in the assignment of moral education to schools and the warning given to schoolteachers against any attempt to teach morality. Gabriel Moran, however, gives an affirmative answer to both these questions, pointing out that his understanding of a lifelong moral development has little in common with Kohlberg's theory of moral development. In relation to teaching morality, Moran

does not begin with classroom instruction, but rather points to the way in which parents, friends, colleagues and others teach morality.

The discomfort concerning the notion of teaching morality discloses a perplexity regarding the very idea of teaching. There is a well-founded suspicion that teaching is an unavoidably immoral act, relying as it does on an unequal relationship between adult and child. Therefore, another question begs consideration: how does one teach morally? In order to address this problem, it is helpful to step back from classroom teaching and examine the meaning of teaching in more ordinary circumstances.

Teaching Morally

Aware that the etymological meaning of the verb *to teach* is to *show how*, Moran states that teaching, understood as showing someone how to do something, does not immediately suggest moral conflict.[100] Teaching is a particular kind of gift, one that evokes a personal response. The universe, in offering daily gifts, is the most extensive teacher. The human person can accept or reject these gifts of nature. The potential for moral conflict begins when moving from the cosmos as teacher to the human community as teacher. As a human being, each person is in a teaching-learning relation with the human family and, therefore, cannot reject being taught. The full emergence of the moral problem occurs when an individual takes on the role of teacher. The person willing to take on this role must examine the circumstances under which he or she can authentically teach. Attention must be paid to the different forms of teaching and the language appropriate to each form. Only then is it possible to teach morally, and only then is it possible to teach morality. This is where the category of *responsibility* comes to the fore.

Responsibility: Teaching is moral when it is responsible. The central characteristic of the human being is to respond or to answer. To be responsible is to respond to whomever and whatever we are related. Therefore, it is central to all morality.

In order to explore the dimensions of responsibility, it is necessary to distinguish between *responsible to* and *responsible for*. According to Moran, we are not responsible for other people, but we are responsible for things. For example, we are responsible for nature, for the earth, for things that cannot decide their fate, but are dependent on human responsibility. The confusion surrounding what people are *responsible for* is linked to the failure to ask 'to what or to whom' are we responsible? The answer is 'everyone and everything'. While it is not possible to embrace the entire universe at any given moment, responsibility requires an attitude of openness so that we might learn from any source that presents itself. Moral judgment helps us choose from the multiplicity of responses available to us. How, therefore, does one act responsibly? 'I am *responsible for* being *responsible to* the truth available to me. My *responsibility to* is limitless, while my *responsibility for* is tightly circumscribed.'[101]

It is important to remember that the category of responsibility is not confined to the human world. Indeed, *responsibility* is the category that provides the primary connection between the human and nonhuman. The human person is responsible to the entire nonhuman world and prior to that, is responsible for his or her actions, together with the consequences of those actions throughout the nonhuman world. In this regard, human responsibility is a three-dimensional term. People have the ability to listen, with varying degrees of attention, to evaluate and reflect upon their previous responses, and to give some or all of their energy to the activity of answering.

A responsible morality, therefore, is a relational morality in the sense of being aware of the many relations that touch our lives. This is the point where religion can play an important role in morality. Religion, understood as the expression of the covenant that exists between the Creator and creation, is a relational activity. Its concern is that none of the important relations in life are lost. Through the narrative descriptions of parable, proverb and epic poetry, each religious tradition reminds men and women 'of their many relations on this earth and their relation to powerful forces beyond earth.'[102]

Response, in a responsible morality, is to everyone and everything. It is to every reality in accordance with its rightful place in the universe. Almost all situations evoke a variety of appropriate responses. Although a responsible morality is insistent on what ought not to be done, it is not a set of directives telling us how to behave. 'It is a living with respect for what birth, past human lives, and the present nurturing environment provide for our response.'[103]

Trans-natural: Teaching is moral when it is *trans-natural.* By this is meant that morality for the human person is at once both natural and more than natural. 'The central moral issue is how to go beyond the natural without going contrary to it.'[104] One does not have a choice about participating in this scheme. It is an inherent human condition, a factor illustrating why the human being is unavoidably a moral animal. Trans-natural is one more way of illustrating Moran's description of the moral and educative process, that is, the reshaping of life's forms, forms that we influence for better or for worse through transforming action.

The central concern of morality is now apparent. The vocation of every human person is not to oppose the natural, but to go beyond it. Morally good activity is in accordance with nature; the natural is not rejected or destroyed. The human vocation is a gentle, non-violent transformation open to the possibilities of improving the natural. In this respect, the use of the term *trans-natural* points to all aspects of the non-natural that are not unnatural. The distinction between non-natural and unnatural paves the way for articulating the foundation of morality: 'what is unnatural is immoral.'[105] Put more succinctly, anything that opposes or destroys the natural is morally wrong.

Private/Public: Teaching is moral when it is private/public. To teach morally is to relate the private inner self with the large public world. No teacher, or anyone else for that matter, has the right to intrude upon the centre of another person's soul. The teacher, rather, shows how, but the onus of response lies with the student. The process of teaching-learning can only take place when the response comes from within. When this occurs, the student has a sense of responsibility for his or her own learning, as well as a responsibility to the teaching.

Teaching Morality

With the teaching of morality, the *moral* moves from being a quality of teaching to the object of teaching. As we saw earlier, morality is always being taught in showing someone how to live. Indeed, every academic subject in the classroom setting has a moral dimension, albeit an implicit one. When morality itself is taught as an academic subject, it becomes the explicit object of teaching.

Following a path similar to teaching morally, the teaching of morality begins with the cosmos as a whole. 'The world and all of the great forces within the world teach both greatness and limitation to human aspirations.'[106] The animals also teach about good and bad activity. At another level, there is a moral wisdom inherent in the human community, a wisdom that individuals must come face to face with in learning morality.

Morality is taught by each of the forms of education described in the above theme on education – family, school, work and leisure. Morality is taught daily in the family setting, with the lesson varying in accordance with the age of the learner. The family is the primary moral teacher by virtue of the fact that it provides the basis of good and evil in the life of the individual.

The school setting, like that of the family, teaches primarily by example. Indeed, the school can be regarded as a moral community that illustrates how virtue is practised. It differs from family, however, by having a broader range of examples, manifested through other students, and through the lives of the adult population working in the school. 'The chief barometer of what the adults are teaching the children is how the adults interact with each other.'[107] As a central community in the lives of children, the school, in its total environment of space, arrangements and interrelations, is the main teacher of morality.

Once a person leaves school, his or her work becomes an important teacher of morality. One's way of life is shaped by the kind of work one does, and the way in which it is done. Most work situations carry the potential to be reshaped through friendliness and helpfulness, thereby contributing to social improvement. Indeed, the manner in which work is carried out can teach invaluable lessons regarding the human community and service to fellow human beings. Almost every work environment provides good and bad examples of morality from which one can learn. The quality of moral development is dependent upon one's response to both teachers.

Moran's fourth educational form – leisure – takes place throughout the course of one's life, but predominates in the latter part of life. The moral teaching that began in infancy and continued throughout school and work will, hopefully, bring some wisdom and moral integrity in old age. Now life's earlier teaching is challenged and the individual's receptivity to life, including death, developed. The person who morally develops into old age possesses a morality of wisdom that manifests itself through lack of attachment to any worldly good. Throughout life, peoples' leisure activities bring them down one of two moral paths. They either become selfish or become more compassionate toward human and nonhuman life. This path leads them to reach out to both the old and the young in society.

Teaching Morality in the Classroom
Gabriel Moran raises two questions concerning the issue of teaching morality in the classroom: (1) does teaching morality

in the classroom throw any light on the teaching of other subjects in the classroom setting? (2) does the part undertaken by the classroom in teaching morality relate in any way to the teaching of morality in and by other educational settings?

Much of the academic world believes that it is impossible or illegitimate to teach morality in a classroom. Can one teach something that is private, subjective and lacking in definitive answers? Moran's belief is that *morality* is an inadequate name for the academic teaching of morality and suggests the term *ethics* as being more appropriate. What worries him when people reject the idea of teaching morality in a classroom is not their assumptions about morality, but what they understand by the meaning of the verb *to teach*. 'The question is whether the main confusion pertains to teaching morality/ethics or to teaching mathematics, science, literature and history.'[108]

Modern ethics, unfortunately, has been construed around how human beings treat each other and how they treat property. 'The division of ethics into individual and social exemplifies and solidifies the bias'.[109] Even when attempts are made to broaden an individualistic ethic to include human groups, the nonhuman world is still not recognised. Ethics is essentially and indispensably a human affair.

The classroom is not a place where people are told the truth. It is a place for a certain kind of conversation, a place for conversing about the nature of conversation. Ambiguity resides in the formulation of every question and every problem. To teach morality is to adopt a questioning stance about any yes or no answer to a complex problem. The teacher's task, therefore, is to postulate a dual perspective: (1) the truth about the position of the topic under discussion insofar as it is drawn from the riches of human history and geography; (2) the inadequacy of the proposed position since it can always be improved upon. The teacher and the student always have more to learn. The ethics teacher is now no different from the teacher of other subjects.

The academic teaching of ethics entails showing a student how to employ a language of morality in a way that can improve understanding. It is 'to provide the language to think clearly, comprehensively, and consistently about the moral life.'[110] Attention to language may seem to many to be an ineffective way to deal with morality since it is deemed that the purpose of teaching morality is to enable people to live better lives. The key, however, lies in attending to the rest of education in morality at the same time that one is directly engaged in teaching ethics in a classroom. To the degree that the rest of a person's education is effective, 'the teaching-learning of ethics will make a moral contribution to that education.'[111] If, however, the opposite is the case, then the teaching-learning of ethics is unlikely to make any difference. It cannot be expected that the virtues of love, care, honesty and discipline will be produced through the teaching of ethics.

The teacher of ethics puts the language of the student in conversation with the wisest minds available. This does not present a choice of talk and action. Rather, the choice entails the kind of talk to be used. In this regard, the ethics teacher must insist upon the use of academic criticism as the most appropriate language for the classroom. 'Teaching ethics means finding the formulas or inarticulate fragments that students have, and trying to improve that language'.[112]

The task of ethics is to challenge the assumptions of the various forms of education in our lives – family, work and leisure activities. The teaching of ethics is the logical outcome of teaching anything in the classroom. It is a modest part in the overall teaching of morality, and it is what keeps education in morality 'from beginning either neutral techniques or conformity to rules'.[113] The task of education, whether or not it is prefixed by the adjective *moral*, is to enhance human life. This includes the relationships between all human people, as well as the relations between the human and the nonhuman.

A Model of Education Towards Adulthood

The synthesis of education and teaching, including moral education, takes place in educating towards adulthood. Adulthood is a lifelong goal, one to which we continually aspire. Adulthood can be referred to as psychological, social and religious maturity. In religious language, it represents the Kingdom of God.

In proposing a model for education towards adulthood, it is interesting to note four contemporary understandings of the word *adult* operative in the English language today.[114] First, the word *adult* is used synonymously with pornographic, with the term *adult* being prefixed to such words as movies and entertainment. While many would dismiss this first meaning as unimportant, this use of the word *adult* has grown rapidly in recent years and is universally understood.

Second, the word *adult* connotes a chronological age or biological point of development. Although this is the clearest meaning of the four, some ambiguity exists between biological time and chronological time. Discrepancies abound concerning the precise stage when people become adults. What is evident is that two stages of life are characterised by society – adult and child.

Relying on psychosocial criteria, the third meaning of *adult* measures the ability of a person to think rationally, objectively and be productive in the work force. In this understanding, becoming adult marks the end of a radical dependence on others, and is manifested in the individual's ability to think, organise, judge and work.

Finally, the word *adult* pertains to the ideally mature person, capable of working towards integration and reconciliation with the world. This meaning of adulthood is characterised through the synthesis of what is often considered to be opposites. The result is maturity and wholeness of being.

The third and fourth understandings of the word *adult* represent two contrasting ideals of adulthood implicit in contemporary culture. In this regard, it is interesting to note the direction education takes in accordance with each ideal. In the third meaning of adulthood, the adult is understood as a rational and independent individual. The educational ideal governed by this understanding of adulthood presents a choice between the child and the adult, between the restrictive, dependent school-based learning of the child and the self-directed, independent learning of the adult. Such an educational system understands the purpose of education to be self-actualisation.

By way of contrast, the fourth meaning of adulthood offers an educational ideal that is concerned with the individual's development in the context of his or her environment. The choice in this educational system lies between 'authoritarian forms of organisation that segregate by age, sex and other categories and a community-based education in which people grow in interdependence.'[115] This meaning of adulthood calls for a model of education that is inclusive of both adults and children, inviting all to grow together towards 'an adulthood that is mature, wise and integral.'[116]

It is interesting to note that an educational model for the fourth meaning of adulthood is not to bring something new into existence. Rather, the task is to search for a more adequate language to describe what is already there. Current educational language, where school is seen as *the* form of education, reflects the third meaning of adulthood. However, Moran's understanding of education as lifelong and lifewide is to honour the fourth meaning of adulthood. In naming the key life forms that educate – family, schooling, work and leisure – it is possible to break through age segregation by opening up these educational possibilities to everyone. 'Everyone at any age needs the support of family/community, everyone needs work, and everyone needs retreat.'[117] What is needed, therefore, is an educational model that is an interplay of family, schooling, work and leisure across the generations. Only when this occurs can people be educated towards psychological, social and religious maturity.

Conclusion

The *Meaning and Forms of Education*, the *Meaning and Forms of Teaching* and *Moral Education and Educating Morally* reveal the essence of Moran's thought in relation to religious education. While all three themes are pertinent, it is important not to regard them in isolation, but rather as forming the overall design of religious education. Individually, they are challenging; together, they are powerful. Both take place within the four social forms of family, schooling, work and leisure and both invite people on a journey towards psychological, social and religious maturity, that is, on a journey toward the Kingdom of God.

Chapter 3

A PARADIGM SHIFT:

EDUCATION
– THE OVERALL FRAMEWORK

Throughout this book, I have drawn attention to the absence of a field of religious education, I have sought to bring about linguistic clarity by exploring the meaning of key words through the eyes of Gabriel Moran and I continue to call, like many others before me, for an adequate theory of religious education. The story thus far involved an exploration and critique of the ecclesiastical language used to design and control the meaning of religious education. This first language of religious education comprised the two components of theology and catechetics/Christian education. The result was that religious education was reduced to the language of the Church. It was equated with catechetics in the Catholic tradition and with Christian education in Protestant circles. Catechetics and Christian education became a kind of practical theology. The task now is to continue the conversation with Gabriel Moran and to show that the term *religious education* has a broader meaning than either catechetics or Christian education.

An Educational Framework for Religious Education
The aim of this chapter is to present an educational framework in an effort to open dialogue within and beyond the Churches. Such a framework necessitates an attempt to create a new field of religious education for which there is, as yet, no adequate

language. What is needed is a language that honours both the religious and the educational in life, a language that would truly be worthy of the title *religious education*. Such a language of religious education would comprise respect for the concrete, particular and, indeed, oftentimes mysterious practices of the religious life. Secondly, the critical capacity of the mind would be applied to the study, understanding, and teaching of religion. Religion should challenge education rather than find its own niche within it. Education and religion need one another. Education needs the challenge of religion in order not to close in on itself and religion needs education so that the Christian Churches preserve within themselves some of the elements of a religious education. This paradigmatic shift recognises that religious education is found at the intersection of religion and education. What is truly envisaged in the intersection of religion and education is a religious education that (a) from the *educational* stance would challenge the quality and purpose of all education and (b) from the *religious* angle would challenge existing religious institutions. This reflects a post-modern sensibility in recognising the contemporary religious upheaval. There is a new opportunity today to insert religion into an *educational* setting so that the negative effects of religion may be diminished and, at the same time, religion may be enabled to be central to life.

Any attempt to break open the language barrier of the Church must contrast two meanings of religious education, one whose roots are deeply embedded in Christianity, the other whose meaning is deeper and broader. These two meanings can be described as follows:

1 Officials of a church indoctrinate children to obey an official church.

2 The whole religious community educates the whole religious community to make free and intelligent religious decisions vis-à-vis the whole world.[1]

In striving to distinguish between these two meanings of religious education, it is important to note that the first meaning contains an inner consistency comprising agent, action, recipient and desired result. Being clearly identified with 'catechesis' in the Roman Catholic tradition and 'Christian education' in the Protestant tradition, this first meaning provides too narrow a framework in which to work. The second meaning, however, has every right to be called religious education.

The second meaning of religious education recognises and acknowledges the community as being both the agent and the recipient of education, with education taking place within the total life of the body. Mutuality becomes the hallmark of education and education is no longer understood as that which happens to children of a certain age within a school setting. Rather, education is for each individual throughout his or her life.

In practice, this understanding of religious education varies in accordance with a person's stage of development. Human experience becomes the connecting link between all stages of growth, with the individual continually adapting and realigning oneself with the environment. Religious education is community based and is 'conceptualised and practised from the reference point of adulthood', that is, psychological, social and religious maturity. [2]

The understanding and practice of religious education from the stance of adulthood is illustrative of the fact that school should never be the only forum for religious education. While the school does contribute to the formation of an intellectually religious person, religious attitudes and values are primarily learned in the community. The function of the religious community is to demonstrate a life into which the child can grow. In this respect, it can be seen that religious education, as it matures towards adulthood, brings together the best of education and the best of religion. It is that which takes place at the intersection of religion and education. In order for this to occur, however, it is necessary to distinguish between some key terms.

Some Critical Distinctions

In order to arrive at a consistent and comprehensive meaning of religious education, some linguistic distinctions are crucial. Central to this reflection lies the necessity to distinguish between three sets of terms: (1) education and school; (2) Christian and religious; (3) religious education and Christian education.

Education and School: While almost all writers on education would argue that the words *education* and *school* are not synonymous, in practice these terms are frequently used interchangeably, with the assumption that education is owned by the school. Such an assumption places an unwarranted burden on the school, as well as serving to exclude other forms of education. It is vital to acknowledge that schooling, while it is extremely important, is only one form of education, and that several *non-schooling* forms of education are in existence. This twofold principle would be particularly beneficial to religion since the teaching of religion in the school classroom does not nurture the practice of a religious way of life, and religious education is not the exclusive task of schoolteachers. It is essential, therefore, that a definition of religious education would include such factors as family life, prayer and social action.

Christian and Religious: In a similar way, it is important to note that the terms *Christian* and *religious* are not synonymous. However, writers in this field frequently allow the religious to be absorbed by the Christian, a movement that serves to put Christianity on a pedestal and regard it as superior to non-Christian religions. In this regard, it is important to remember that Christianity is vitally important as one form or several forms of the religious life and that it is only one form or several forms of the many.[3] The duty of every individual, therefore, is to differentiate between the multiple forms of religious and one form of religiousness, for example, Christian.

Religious Education and Christian Education: To use the terms *religious education* and *Christian education* synonymously serves to exclude Judaism, as well as education within other religious traditions. Indeed, such usage of the terms diminishes the role of religious education in general since 'a religion can be "transmitted" today only in the context of a continuing conversation with other religions.'[4] A second reason against using the terms synonymously concerns the fact that the term *Christian education* is used exclusively by the Protestant tradition, thereby also excluding Roman Catholics. Catholics, on the other hand, seems to have a monopoly on the word *catechetics*, a term steeped in history, but which has only been popularised since the Second Vatican Council. While Protestants are guilty of equating religious education and Christian education, the current language of the Roman Catholic tradition cannot be assumed to be the only possible language of religious education.

In distinguishing between these three sets of terms, the overriding intention is to promote a theory of religious education that cannot be reduced to the language of the Church. Religion and education need to be consistent and complementary partners. Religion's role is to challenge education and enable it to rediscover the richness of what it is to be *religious*. Conversely, the scene is changed when the affairs of religion are brought into the educational framework – the true essence of education is revealed.

It is now possible to establish some precepts necessary for a field of religious education.

1   Rather than comprising abstract or diluted generalities, the religious aspect of religious education must be concrete, distinctive and unparalleled. Such a maxim can be provided by an educational setting in which religious doctrines are reconstructed with reverence, intelligence and patience.

2   The establishment of a grand synthesis is not the aim of religious education. Rather, religious education seeks to foster greater appreciation and understanding of one's own religious life, as well as that of other people.

3   A third axiom for a field of religious education is the provision of a place in which the past can be handed on in

the form of ritual and historical study. In this regard, it is important to note that, while the teaching of religion in the school environment offers an invaluable contribution to religious education, it is inadequate in its ability to sustain a religious life. In sum, the encounter between religion and education is likely to result in two things:

a   a transformation of the new religious group from within, resulting in changed institutions and in new methods for transmitting the religious life to the next generation.

b   a conversation with other religious groups that will eventually lead to increased   tolerance and mutual understanding.[5]

In his attempt to conceptualise an advocated meaning of religious education, Gabriel Moran, as we have seen, posits two settings – 'school' and 'laboratory' – the latter comprising all of life and in particular areas such as family/community life, work and leisure activity. While not equating education and school, he argues that the Churches need good schools where religion can be taught and studied. Two distinct religious orientations exist within the school setting. One concerns the study of religion from the perspective of a specific tradition. The second involves a certain distancing from one's tradition and involves the study of religion in an intersubjective manner. The latter approach, on its own, is inadequate but, combined with the first, is an essential ingredient for contemporary religious education.

Within the laboratory setting there are, as we know, three main orientations to learning: the family/community, the work site and the 'retreat'. In each of these settings the religious question can organically emerge. George Albert Coe, for example, pointed to the 'measureless potential of the family as an agency of Christian education.'[6] While Moran agrees that the family is an essential element in religious education, he also states that it is very important not to romanticise it. C. Ellis Nelson also shares this view. Acknowledging the family as a very important agent in communicating Christian faith, he believes that a system of Christian nurture cannot be based on the family alone 'because the family is more an agent of culture and society than it is an independent unit.'[7] The family, therefore, needs to be provided with communal settings if it is to be effective in its task. There is a need for learning within families, learning between children and adults of all ages, learning between the very old and the very young, learning between families and all institutions of society.

Liturgy provides us with another example. The educational possibilities of the liturgy are endless, but liturgy needs to be a family / community affair that is related to social action. Liturgy, if it is allowed to blossom, has the potential to furnish all of education with a sacramental character. A contemplative attitude, which is developed through quiet time and space, is complementary to liturgy and resides at the heart of all good education.

In this conceptualisation, Moran outlines some principles concerning the meaning of religious education: (1) Religious education is pertinent to all of life and to all of education. (2) The artistic and the cultic are very important dimensions of religious education, thereby diminishing the role of the rational and discursive world of the school. (3) Religious education ought to be a way of knowledge rather than a study of faith. In other words, it ought to be the practice of a religious way of life. Education, therefore, can make an important contribution to the deficient field of religious education by way of knowledge and practice.

Within this understanding, religious education may be described as the interplay of two complementary, but differing, aims: (1) to teach religion and (2) to teach to be religious. It is akin to the vocation and avocation of Parker J. Palmer:

> My vocation is the spiritual life, the quest for God, which relies on the eye of the heart. My avocation is

education, the quest for knowledge, which relies on the eye of the mind.[8]

To teach religion involves the understanding of one's own religion, as well as the religion of others. This takes place in an academic setting and is the model of religious education prevalent in the United Kingdom where religion is taught as an academic subject on the school curriculum. The teaching of religion in an academic setting is also contributing to the changing shape of religious education in the Republic of Ireland. To teach to be religious, on the other hand, involves formation and nurturance in a way of life. This takes place in the family and in the parish through the experiences of community and worship, and is the understanding of religious education found in the United States of America. These two natures or faces of religious education are related, but must be clearly distinguished.

Two Aims or Faces of Religious Education
The two aims of religious education – to teach to be religious and to teach to understand religion – are related, distinct, and of equal importance. Within this understanding, religious education comprises two forms, two processes, and two aims – all of which take place within a multitude of settings. It is interesting to note that both activities are described as 'teaching people'.[9] This does not mean that the person doing the teaching is a person with the title 'teacher'. Rather, the ultimate source of the teaching is the human community and the nonhuman environment.

A second noteworthy aspect in the distinction between the two aims concerns the difference between the noun 'religion' and the adjective 'religious'. The modern use of the word 'religion' is ambiguous in that it can be used to refer to a subject on the school curriculum or it may allude to a set of practices carried out by a particular religious group. The adjective 'religious', on the other hand, reveals the particular way in which one can be religious. This ambiguity concerning religion is advantageous to the extent that it points to the inner connection between 'teaching people to be religious in a particular way' and 'teaching people religion'. These aims are not simply parallel processes in which disparate groups engage. Rather, one or other process can predominate in the life of an individual at any particular moment.

A Word on Teaching

In discussing the aims of religious education, the question of perspective is pivotal. The use of the verb 'to teach' in both aims reveals that two contrasting forms of teaching are required in order to carry them out. Teaching, as we noted earlier, is an activity in which every human being and some nonhumans engage. Teaching involves showing someone how to do something. Put more succinctly, it means showing someone how to live, which eventually includes how to die. Such a comprehensive understanding stands in stark contrast to the narrow meaning of teaching prevalent in today's world, that of furnishing children with explanations. While providing reasons and explanations is very important, other languages of teaching must also be included. This is where the three groups or families of languages espoused by Moran – the homiletic, therapeutic and academic – are indispensable.

First Aim/Face: To teach to be religious – teaching the way
The first face of religious education is akin to the notion of religious socialisation as articulated by Ellis Nelson,[10] Westerhoff [11,12] and Marthaler[13]. It concerns the initiation, formation and socialisation of each new generation who will carry out the practices, ritual and mission of the religious group. This work of forming people to be religious and behaving in a religious manner is carried on by the adult members of the community. The religious community, however, needs a boundary in order to provide intimacy, support and identity for its members.

The importance of socialisation is highlighted by the emphasis C. Ellis Nelson places on the manner in which culture/religion influences a person's life. If a child is surrounded by religion from the moment of birth, religion shapes that person's selfhood long before he or she becomes self-consciously aware. 'What is unknown', he writes, 'is that culture is internalised in persons and institutionalised in society. Culture is the meaning of life that is transmitted to others, especially children.'[14] The world-view of a particular way of being religious is mediated directly to children by those who nurture and socialise them and becomes an integral part of their self-understanding. 'Imitation is the method by which a person appropriates the style of life of the group in which he comes to selfhood.'[15] The values imbibed by young children, therefore, are, to a large extent, an extension of the values of the nurturing group. In this regard, Ellis Nelson writes:

> The child does not come into self-awareness and then discover culture; he finds and defines himself in a particular culture..the appropriation of his parents' way of seeing and living is built deep into his personality – partly consciously – and it permeates his whole being. [16]

The symbols that give meaning and explanations of life, therefore, play a very important role in the transmission of a religious way of life to each individual.

John H. Westerhoff (III) advocates a process of intentional religious socialisation. By religious socialisation he means 'a process consisting of lifelong formal and informal mechanisms, through which persons sustain and transmit their faith (world view, value system) and life style'.[17] While he acknowledges the major influence of family and peers, his primary interest in calling for *intentional religious socialisation* lies in the socialisation that takes place in faith communities. Without a community of faith supporting and transmitting the family's

Christian vision, the task facing religious socialisation is very difficult. 'An intentional community of faith remains the essential key to religious socialisation.'[18] The great challenge, therefore, is to enable local churches to become religious communities in which the Christian faith can be transmitted.

Berard L. Marthaler enters the conversation by distinguishing between faith and belief.[19] Faith is a personal response to gift whose meaning is mediated by specific beliefs. The socialisation, therefore, of a person into a particular religious tradition is more concerned with beliefs than faith. In this regard, he is in agreement with Westerhoff that 'faith cannot be taught by any method of instruction and that religions can only be taught.'[20] The seeds of faith can be awakened, nourished and developed by catechesis or education in faith. The role of catechesis is to unearth the mysteries lying beneath the surface of everyday life, as well as to recount the story and transmit the wisdom of a particular tradition. In this regard, he names three objectives of the socialisation model of religious education: (1) growth in personal faith, (2) religious affiliation and (3) the maintenance and transmission of a religious tradition.

In teaching to be religious, the aim is to teach people to be religious in a particular way, that is, in the way of Judaism, Catholicism or Islam, to name but a few. The object here is singular – 'the practice of one concrete set of activities that exclude other ways of acting', with the teacher comprising the community and the environment.[21] Although the parish is deemed to be the place where people are taught to be religious in a Catholic way, it is the liturgical community that forms the heart of this teaching. In this setting, energies for social justice flow from common worship and individual prayer. 'The experience of prayer and the overflow into moral engagement with today's world is what forms the person as Christian.'[22] It is, to use an ecclesiastical term, the way in which *diakonia* is manifested in parish life, that is, preaching by service resulting in works of justice.

Westerhoff and Kennedy Neville strongly emphasise the role of the Christian community in transmitting its vision and way of life to young people, an emphasis receiving increasing attention today. Their contention is that religious education must be 'centred on the life and work of the community of faith.'[23] People are socialised 'by the space and ecology in which they live.'[24] The local church community offers an endless hidden curriculum to all members, one that is a powerful teaching force. In this regard, Westerhoff calls for the life and structures of the faith community to be renewed and suggests that it begins with the adult members of the community. Not detracting from the primordial role of the family as the first and powerful agency of socialisation, he, like Moran, notes that their efforts will be ineffective without the support of a vibrant faith community. Furthermore, people require the experience of being part of a group that celebrates the presence and action of God in a sacramental fashion.

The first aim of religious education begins at birth and engages the homiletic and therapeutic families of teaching languages. It is these languages of teaching, together with nonverbal forms of teaching, that show people what it means to live in accordance with a religious way of life. From the first moments of life, a child is taught by an adult community to be religious. Through persistent learning, continued demonstrations of care and compassion and ongoing celebrations of a living liturgy, the adult community provides the young with what they most need. Indeed, liturgical worship is the predominant form of teaching in the religious community and it is within this practice that the first family of languages – storytelling, lecturing and preaching – is embedded. Religious rituals also contain a wide range from the second family of languages in the form of praise, thanks, confessing of sins and mourning the dead. The third family of languages, the academic, plays a limited role in teaching people to be religious.

In summary, it can be said that teaching the way means showing people how to live and how to die through the embodiment of a set of beliefs, symbols and actions. All of these link people to the abiding religious questions of 'Where do I come from?', 'Where am I going and why?' It is about educating members of the Church to take responsibility for continuing the mission of Jesus, the Christ, in the world today.

Second Aim/Face: Teaching to understand religion
The second face of religious education is mostly a matter of the mind and involves the provision of an understanding of religion, including one's own religion. An openness to understand is an antidote to the tendency to attack, belittle, condemn or dismiss what may, on the surface, seem bizarre or absurd. The test of genuine understanding will be gauged by whether or not one is ready to listen attentively, reflect calmly, and judge fairly.

The second aim of religious education is to teach people to understand religion. In this process the aim is 'to understand'. This activity necessitates a double conversation: the dialogue between the major world religions and the dialogue of religion(s) and contemporary culture. While such an understanding of religion can take place anywhere, the classroom has been intentionally established as the ideal setting for this process. The teaching of religion in the school context is an essential component of the field of religious education. Mindful of the fact that teaching involves showing someone how to do something, the responsibility for showing someone how to employ words and concepts in order to understand religion falls on the school. In this situation, the student is enabled to ascertain a deeper level of enquiry than would be available outside the classroom. Scholars, like Gabriel Moran, argue for the inclusion of religion in the school setting, stating that 'school is precisely where religion belongs.'[25] Religion is an academic category. More precisely, it is 'an idea and a method posited by scholars', indicating the intention to exercise the mind in comprehending not only one's own religious tradition, but also that of other peoples.[26]

Showing a person how to use words and concepts in order to undertake the study of religion involves a fourfold approach.[27] (1) The teacher must intelligibly present the available material. (2) The teacher must enable the religious text to act as mediator between the community of another era and the community of today. (3) In order to facilitate the understanding of religious meaning, the teacher must participate in the meaning to a certain degree. In other words, the teacher must step into the shoes of the writer and perceive the world from that perspective. (4) The teacher must draw upon the experience of students and teachers.

Unfortunately, in the United States, the task of teaching people to understand religion has been relegated, almost entirely, to religious institutions, a burden that is too heavy to carry. The parish is not well designed for this task. Rather, its assignment is to teach people to be religious in a Catholic way. In the Republic of Ireland, for example, the situation is reversed, with the full chore of teaching religion being the sole task of the school.

While the word *religion* in the second aim is written in the singular, its object is plural. It begins from the perspective of one's own religion, but entails comparisons with other religions, a factor that leads to a better understanding of one's own religion. The third family of teaching languages is dominant here with teaching taking place through dialectical discussion and academic criticism. Although this family of languages is central to the second aim, it does draw its content from the other two families.

Comparing and contrasting the two aims
A complete contrast between the two faces of religious education would involve describing the who, what, how, where and why of this enterprise. Indeed, the recipients of religious education will vary according to each face of religious education. In the first type, the recipients are enquirers or initiants of a religious community. Here the focus is very

particular: this group of people either desires to be, or is socialised into the way of life and ritual practice of the faith community. In this regard, most religious bodies, such as the Christian, Jewish and Muslim faiths, concentrate on children. By adopting the premises of modern education, many religious groups understand religious education as an activity that begins at the age of four or five, thereby neglecting the most formative time in children's lives. A lifelong education, however, would begin at birth or before it and continue until death. If one follows this path, it implies that the religious body shows special concern for the parents of young children.

In the second face of religious education, *understanding religion*, the recipients span the whole of the human life-cycle, from young child to older adult, taking account of the fact that the capacity to understand religion develops gradually over many years. The ability to exercise critical judgments about one's own religion in relation to the religion of others demands a certain maturity. In this regard, to place so much emphasis on religious education in the primary school years does not make sense. Furthermore, since some basis of comparison is necessary to understand any phenomenon, a manageable diversity is desirable among the recipients of the second kind of religious education. The desire of Catholic leaders to have members of their church understand their own religion before encountering other religions is understandable, but it is important to remember that understanding involves comparison. J.S. Dunne concurs with this position in advocating that by crossing over to other religions one comes back to one's own with much enrichment.[28]

This distinction made between the two types of religious education does not compartmentalise people into one or either category. Each recipient needs access to both kinds of religious education at the appropriate time in his or her life. It is possible, or likely, that there are times when both faces of religious education operate simultaneously, but, at some moments in life, one or other is likely to dominate. For example, in early childhood, socialisation into the faith community necessarily takes precedence; in late adolescence there is usually a tendency to resist formation within the community, but if this tension is carefully facilitated, the mature adult can hold the two kinds of religious education in fruitful tension.

Despite the different forms of religious agency that are involved in the twofold religious enterprise, *religious education* already serves for both realities in different parts of the world. Indeed, the world needs both faces of religious education. It is not necessary for every religious educator to focus on both faces of this discipline, 'but while concentrating on one kind', Moran writes, 'the educator has to be aware of another aspect to the work.'[29] On the one hand, religious commitment does not preclude the importance of understanding religion and, on the other hand, scholars benefit from a feel for religious practice.

A religious education that embraces these contrasting activities of *formation* and *understanding* is threatened by opposite dangers. On one side, there is the danger that those who engage in a purely academic examination of religion would take over the meaning of the term, leaving religious bodies bereft of a link between internal cultural formation and the outside world's educational efforts in religion. This problem is associated, primarily, with countries such as Great Britain where the term *religious education,* especially at post-primary level, is usually confined to the designation of a subject taught in state schools. This danger does not exist in the United States and, until recently did not threaten the Republic of Ireland. In the latter case, religion has now become an exam subject on the curriculum of Irish post-primary schools. This carries the danger of limiting religious education to the school setting, thereby encapsulating it in one particular form. The opposite danger exists in the United States where religious education is regarded as an activity proper to a religious body, but illegal in the public school. A framework for a discussion on religion and education is badly needed in the United States. In this regard, the Catholic Church, which fuelled the renewal of the term *religious education* since the Second Vatican Council, needs to be careful not to speak and act as if it owns the term.

It must be acknowledged that the Catholic Church has the right and the duty to preserve its own language. The exclusive association of religious education with catechesis, however, contrasts it to a small and segregated part of the Church's ministry. This confining type of language diminishes the possibility of healthy educational discussion within the Catholic Church, as well as the Church's association and dialogue with other educational bodies.

The words *catechist* and *catechise*, which had their roots in the early Church and in early Protestant history, resurfaced after the Second Vatican Council. The use of these words is valid as a language of intimacy within Catholicism, but it should be kept in tension with language that transcends the Catholic Church. Catechesis, the aim of which is to form people in the Christian way of life, should not be burdened with the assumptions of the classroom. Likewise, academic religious education should not be burdened with the role of catechising. The type of teaching that occurs in the context of a homily or in sacramental preparation may be inappropriate in the classroom. In the academic sector religion is taught whereas the catechetical venture focuses on the formation of people in a Christian way of life.

Gabriel Moran's view of the catechetical as a small, but important, aspect of Catholic religious education is not reflected in Church documents or in most of the writing in this area over the past three decades. He believes that 'the catechetical aspect of the Catholic Church tends to overreach its place within the ministries of the Church.'[30] He disagrees with the statement in *Sharing the Light of Faith* that the tasks of the catechist are 'to proclaim Christ's message, to participate in efforts to develop community, to lead people to worship and prayer, and to motivate them to serve others.'[31] Only one of these, the proclamation of the message, clearly belongs to the catechist. Catechesis seems to be overreaching its task and role. This catechetical language needs to be complemented by an educational language. According to Moran, the educational formation of a Catholic rests more on worship and service than on catechetics. 'One learns to be a Catholic', Moran writes, 'by participating in the liturgical life of the community.'[32] According to this way of thinking, if educational reform is to be successful in the Church, it must shift its concentration beyond catechisms and textbooks. While one might subscribe to this view theoretically, the reality in most parishes is that liturgy is not the primary place for faith formation.

Conclusion

The marriage of the two aims of religious education takes place in the person of the learner. Although one or other aim takes precedence at different stages throughout a person's life, it is hoped that every human person has the opportunity to engage in both aims. Like all education, religious education begins from the first moment of life, with the family being the natural setting for this first phase. As the child matures and develops, varying institutional contexts are available commensurate to the needs of age. While the first aim of religious education predominates in early childhood, the second aim is likely to take centre stage in adolescence as the facility to form abstractions occurs through conceptual and linguistic development. Both aims of religious education ought to characterise adult life.

In sum, religious education may be described as:

> Teaching people religion with all the breadth and depth of intellectual excitement one is capable of and teaching people to be religious with all particularity of the verbal and nonverbal symbols that place us on the way.[33]

Chapter 4

THE FAMILY AS RELIGIOUS EDUCATOR

Chapter Three witnessed the paradigm shift from an ecclesiastical to an educational framework for religious education. In continuity with this thought, the next three chapters will take up the educational forms of family, school and parish and examine their roles in religious education. Beginning with the family, this chapter proposes to examine the unique and different ways in which the family is a lifelong educational form. In order to explore this line of thought, the family will be examined under three different themes: (1) the family as educator, (2) the family as teacher and (3) the family as moral educator. Aware that the family partially embodies the universal value of community, *the family as educator* examines the way in which education takes place through the interplay of communal family relations. *The family as teacher* theme explores the manner in which the family teaches by design, namely, the form in which economics, power and sex are manifested in daily family life. Pertinent to this theme are the homiletic and therapeutic languages of teaching in which the family engages. Authentic teaching, however, always includes a moral dimension. The *family as moral educator* illustrates how the family educates morally all the time through modelling, witnessing and demonstrating a way of life.

The family, as religious educator, engages in many forms of learning. Education within the family takes place in a unique manner and in a way that differs from other educational forms. Current educational language, however, has been constructed in such a way as to eliminate the enormous educational influence of the family. Gabriel Moran challenges this construction and argues 'for at least several thousand years, family has clearly deserved to be called a form of education.'[1] His thesis that contemporary educational language narrowly perceives school as *the* form of education is strongly supported by Margaret M. Sawin who believes that 'our culture is conditioned by schools and other educational institutions to think that learning takes place only within the formal structure of education.'[2] Such a narrow perception of education has served to eclipse the existence of other educational forms, as well as place an unwarranted burden on the school. The problem lies with the absence of a single *bona fide* understanding of education leading to a deficiency in the meaning of the term.

1. The Family as Educator

Throughout this book, I have sought to illustrate that the world of education is not comprised solely of one single form (schooling) but, rather, is made up of a configuration of forms. For the purposes of this chapter, an exploration of some of the prevailing concepts of education is helpful in attempting to arrive at a more comprehensive meaning of the term. It is important to note here that there is no pure meaning of education. Its meaning, rather, is found in the way in which it is used. While definitions of education are plentiful, none seems to capture the essence of the term's full meaning.

Lawrence A. Cremin has defined education as 'the deliberate systematic and sustained effort to transmit, evoke, or acquire knowledge, values, attitudes, skills and sensibilities (and the results of that effort)'.[3] This definition marks his acknowledgment that education generally proceeds via many individuals and institutions – parents, peers, siblings and friends, as well as families, churches, libraries, museums, summer camps, schools and colleges.[4]

Maria Harris criticises Cremin's understanding of education, stating that it 'tends to obscure the existence of other more aesthetically related understandings of education.'[5] Her suggestion to give careful consideration to the aesthetic concepts of education finds resonance in John Dewey's understanding of education as the 'reconstruction and reorganisation of experience' and alludes immediately to the manner in which education makes, creates and forms.[6] Gabriel Moran's criticism of Cremin's definition of education centres on the word 'effort'. 'The standpoint', he writes, 'seems to be that of the individual human teacher: to teach is to intend, to teach is to make an effort and hope for outcomes from the effort.'[7]

By way of contrast, Gabriel Moran offers an understanding of education as the 'reshaping of life's forms with end (meaning) but without end (termination).'[8] Such a description of education reveals that the four life forms of family, schooling, work and leisure are being constantly shaped and reshaped throughout life. This takes place through the various relations encountered within those life forms and through the changing roles that people assume throughout the course of life. Education, therefore, is lifelong. It has no end. In this regard, it is essential to note the two meanings of *end* in the above description of education. In education, life forms are continually being redesigned and reformed with meaning. It is a process that never terminates. Termination makes it impossible to perceive education as lifelong, whereas *end* as *meaning* portrays education as an endless process. These two meanings of *end* need to be held in creative tension. Only when education is described in this way can it be understood as an artistic process of shaping and reshaping life's forms.

The Forms of Education – A recapitulation
Moran's understanding of education as the interaction of life forms with end (meaning) and without end (termination) necessitates a description of the major lifelong and lifewide forms of life. Acknowledging the innumerable social forms that comprise the educational curriculum, he concentrates on four forms with which people interact throughout their lives. Education for every human being begins at conception and is received through the family pattern to which he or she belongs. As the child grows older, the classroom becomes the predominant form of education. Upon entering adulthood, a person is expected to participate in the workforce, and as a retired person, he or she experiences more time for leisure activity. 'Thus', Moran writes, 'family, classroom, job and leisure activity can be viewed as a lifelong sequence, the simplest basis for a theory of education.'[9]

Moran isolates the word 'interaction' as the key to this lifelong sequence and believes that the interaction of family, classroom, job and leisure at every stage of life leads to a more comprehensive theory of education. This understanding of education recognises that, whatever a person's age, any one of the four social forms can take centre-stage, while the other three are present in the background. For example, the family form of education recedes when a child goes to school, although it continues to educate in partnership with the school and in conjunction with job and leisure. Family re-emerges at other points in life, particularly when people become parents and grandparents. In this regard, Moran writes that

> the point of so describing the family in education is not
> to fit each individual's life into a preset pattern but to
> recognise that a person's life is educationally shaped by

familial relations, with variations depending on gender, marital status, parental responsibility, house arrangements, and many other factors.[10]

It is important to note that the educational experiences of family, schooling, job and retirement can, to borrow Dewey's phrase, be educational or miseducational. These life forms are educational to the degree that they embody universal values – that is, the universal values of community, knowledge, work and wisdom. For example, the family, in order to be educational, needs to embody the value of community and, at the same time, requires the complementation of other embodiments, for example, knowledge, work and wisdom. In this regard, Moran points out that family is a partial embodiment of community to the extent that 'no family exhausts the meaning of community; a family needs other families and also non-familial forms of community life.'[11] By this is meant that family will succeed in being a place and experience of community only if, secondarily, it is a place and experience of knowledge, work and wisdom. Education, therefore, may be described as a journey towards community, knowledge, work or wisdom. These are the values that lead us forward to adulthood.

Education within the family
Education within the family takes place in a unique way and in a manner that differs from other educational forms. The family educates, first and foremost, by being a family. Family educates by being a community, and it educates by shaping and reshaping the fragile relationship between family and community. In so doing, it educates its members to live in a larger world.

For Sawin the family is 'the basic social unit of our human world', a 'microcosm of the larger society' and a place where the primary models of every human interaction are encountered: 'love and hate, co-operation and competition, trust and rivalry, harmony and conflict, and many others.'[12] In summarising this influence, Hope Leichter acknowledges the familial setting as the *loci* of a wide range of human experiences, as well as a plethora of educational encounters. Enumerating these experiences, she writes that 'warfare, violence, love, tenderness, honesty, deceit, private property, communal sharing, power manipulation, informed consent, formal status hierarchies, egalitarian decision-making' can all be located within the area of the family.[13] In addition to these experiences, the family provides an assortment of educational encounters ranging from 'conscious systematic instruction to repetitive moment-to-moment influences at the margins of awareness.'[14] It is only when these rich and diverse educational encounters are examined that our contemporary understanding of education can be expanded.

Family education focuses neither on the education of adults only nor on the education of children only. Rather, it concentrates on the education of all family members as a unit. Moran emphasises the multiple forms of education that occur in the family system, noting in particular the complementary educational activities between parents and children. While it is universally accepted that parents educate children, one does not often think in terms of children as educators of parents. However, the very rapid development in information technology gives practical expression to the educative role of children vis-à-vis parents. Yet, the more important forms of a child's educative role occur in a more subtle manner.

Education of Children by Parents: That parents are the major educators of their children is an unavoidable truth. Parents educate their children, not so much by being (schooling) instructors, but by being parents. In this regard, Maria Harris distinguishes between *physical* (religious) education and *storied* (religious) education.[15] The physical education of children begins at the moment of conception and is manifested through the ways in which parents demonstrate care and concern for the child as he or she journeys toward birth. Education continues after birth as the parents welcome and love the child, instilling experiences of warmth, tenderness, care, security, trust. At this stage the child learns, primarily, through his or her body.

Virginia Satir highlights self-worth as the family's most essential contribution to the development of personality and learning patterns in the child. She writes:

> ... I am convinced that the crucial factor in what happens both inside people and between people is the picture of individual worth that each person carries around with him. I am convinced that there are no genes to carry the feeling of worth. It is learned. And the family is where it is learned.[16]

Sawin delineates four tasks in the role of parents as educators of their children: protection, nourishment, guidance and loving. Protection is the first parental act in which parents protect their children *from* everything, doing so *for* their children. The second component of parenting is nourishing where parents nourish and nurture their children. Both protection and nourishing work in such a way as to provide space for children to uncover the true meaning of their identity and to discern the poetry and passion of their hearts. Guidance is the third component where the parent accompanies, directs and conveys knowledge to the child. Finally, none of this is possible without the presence of love. Harris puts it beautifully when she writes that loving means

> that parents offer their children the vast reservoir of their own spirituality and their own adulthood – fragile as these might be – and make their resources of body and mind available to their children for the duration of the child's life.[17]

Education of Parents by Children: Acknowledging the reciprocal relationship between parents and children, Moran draws attention to the education of parents by children, stating that the child 'childs' the parents. Children educate their parents simply by being children, and parents learn about spontaneity, playfulness and novelty from their children. Through their children and their children's association with others, parents learn about child development and strategies of schooling. Indeed, parental involvement in the lives of their children introduces a new world vision where every aspect of the child's activities 'becomes a potential source of education for the parent.'[18]

The journey of the child from conception to adulthood educates parents in the area of child and psychosocial development. At each stage of their child's development parents enter new parental roles as they learn to adjust and readjust to the rapid maturation rate of their child. It is important to note here that the unique and individual character of each child in the family setting offers parents an educative experience that differs from that of their siblings. In this way, the child acts as an educational catalyst and the potential source of education for parents is continuous and lifelong.

Margaret Mead illustrates how rapid social change in a given society affects the educational relationship between one generation and another.[19] Citing the example of children whose experiences differ so markedly from that of their parents and elders, she notices that the elders become immigrants in a foreign world and must, therefore, be educated by their children on how to live in that world. In a similar vein, she draws attention to the educative role of the child as he or she acts as linguistic interpreter for parents on the occasion of the family's move to a new cultural setting. Both of these examples find resonance with children deeply influenced by the media. Their vivid presentation of tastes and styles of thought provide educational opportunities for parents.

Education of Siblings by Siblings: Siblings have a profound educational influence on each other by virtue of the fact that they are likely to spend a lot of time together. While studies to date have shown little concern with the education of siblings by siblings, the potential for such inquiry is great. For example, literature on ordinal position (birth order) 'suggests that siblings may well mediate parental behavior and attitudes within the family.'[20] Thus, the position of individual siblings may have a bearing on the extent of verbal exchange with parents, as well as on the amount and quality of guidance from parents. Siblings, therefore, may act as models and means of evaluation for one another. Although little research has been done on this area, Donald P. Irish contends that 'siblings may serve not only as role models for one another, but also as challengers and stimulators.'[21] Others, however, argue that siblings frequently work out self-definitions with each other.[22]

There are, however, indications of the enormous educational influence siblings have on each another. For example, it is well known that siblings spend a large quantity of time together and share a broad variety of activities. This results in relationships that are intimate and inclusive, with sibling interaction being marked by 'frankness, informality, cohesiveness, intensity, and extensity.'[23] Siblings acquire a sense of social reality from one another, as well as experience in conflict resolution. In addition, they engage one another in daily matters of truth, justice, and responsibility, all the time providing what Irish calls a 'school of mirrors'.[24]

Furthermore, it has been suggested that the manner in which siblings educate one another differs from that of parents. According to Irish, the education of siblings by siblings is frequently more effective than education by adults, particularly when the skills of youth are involved. New situations and childhood problems are often better understood by siblings than by parents. In this regard, siblings may engage in educational functions by being examples for each another in a whole variety of settings.

Education of Parents by Parents: Education within the family also takes place through the relations between husband and wife. A significant factor in the way in which parents educate one another is the changing roles that take place in the family over a period of time. Studies have shown that during the course of adulthood significant shifts occur in definitions of self and meaningful activities.[25] The educational importance of these changes in self-definition become clear when they are regarded in conjunction with the processes of socialisation and anticipatory socialisation.

Literature on the various forms of intermarriage is also indicative of the ways in which parents educate each other in each other's cultural background. Even when little difference exists in the cultural tradition of each parent, parents influence each other in the art of parenting and out of their experiences in non-familial settings. As Leichter puts it, 'encounters outside the family are a vehicle through which parents learn from one another and, in turn, teach their children.'[26]

By way of conclusion, it can be seen that the family educates in a unique and different way. The family educates by being a family and by partially embodying the universal value of community. It educates by recognising and accepting the inestimable gift of family and is, therefore, the primordial educator. No other form of life may have its formative influence.

2. The Family as Teacher

The Catholic tradition has had a long history in acknowledging the role of the family as teacher. This emphasis on the teaching aspect of family life continues to be found in its most recent documents. For example, *Familiaris Consortio* speaks of the family as 'the first school of those social virtues which every society needs.'[27] Teaching within the family takes place in a plurality of ways. It forms a community of persons, serves life, participates in the development of society and, from the ecclesial perspective, shares in the life and mission of the Church. This teaching function of the family pertains to all of its members and, ideally, occurs in an inter-generational fashion. However, the Catholic tradition has never spelt out in adequate detail the manner in which the family teaches.

The indispensable contribution of Gabriel Moran to this conversation is that he elaborates upon the forms in which teaching takes place in the family system. He explores how the family teaches by being a family and illustrates how the quality of this teaching is dependent upon the quality of their lives together. In doing this, he examines the manner in which the family teaches by (a) *design*, that is, in terms of the structure and pattern of family life; and (b) *modelling/performance*, that is, the daily performance of the family models a particular way in which to live. Here the various teaching languages are highlighted, particularly the homiletic and therapeutic, in addition to their role in the performance of the family as teacher. The family also teaches in an academic fashion, particularly when parents engage each other and their children in reflection and academic debate.

The manner in which educational literature employs the verb *to teach* frequently conceals the powerful contribution of the family as teacher. Indeed, this contribution will never be fully recognised as long as teaching is solely associated with what happens in a classroom. Teaching needs to be freed from the fetters that bind it to classroom instruction in order to be understood as an activity that takes place within life's social forms. Only when this occurs will the family form be recognised and accepted as the first great and powerful teacher.

Modern literature on education operates from a further assumption that teaching is an intentional activity. Such an assumption stands in stark contrast to the daily interaction that takes place in family life, an interaction that illustrates how much of the teaching within the familial setting occurs unintentionally. Examples of this can be seen in the various forms of family groupings in existence in today's society. The authoritarian form of family, for example, teaches differently from the family where power is shared on a more equal basis. Similarly, the teaching experienced in one-parent families differs from that experienced by families where both parents are in residence. Families in which both parents work outside the home teach a different lesson from the families in which one parent remains at home. All these examples are illustrative of the fact that whether the lessons learned are good or bad, the family, as an educational form, is the first great teacher.

Teaching by design

The manner in which the family form teaches can be educative or miseducative. In this regard, Moran explores the pattern of family relationships in order to illustrate how the family teaches by design.[28] Exploring what is teaching in the form of family life, his intention is to indicate how these forces can be redesigned so that family members can find a better way to work within the pattern of familial life. The term 'design' may be understood as an attempt 'to capture both the express intent of the human teacher and the material limits of what can be taught.'[29] Contained within the meaning of teaching by design is the desire to shape. Teaching now becomes an activity and the teaching-learning process occurs through doing. In order to teach by design, it is necessary to examine the current design in existence and to propose a redesign in order that the learner may act differently. This is a pattern that can be repeated many times. In showing someone how to do something, therefore, the activity of teaching never separates itself from the metaphor of design.

How can the family teach by design? This question can best be answered by examining the teaching that takes place in a patriarchal form of family and contrasting it to what a more community oriented form of family life teaches. Historically, the structure of the family in Western society was pyramidic in shape, with the flow of power descending from father to mother to child. The father, as head of the household, exercised power over the mother and child, both of whom responded in obedience. Sexual expression was exercised in a similar fashion, with sexual life being controlled by the male

With regard to work, the father was responsible for the family income and for the provision of sustenance for the family. The mother, on the other hand, was occupied with the children and the housework and was, therefore, considered not to work. Because of his position as *bread-earner*, the father was also the one who exercised authority and control in the family. In the event of his absence, this responsibility was passed onto the mother.

Not all families, however, comprise father, mother and children. Factors such as death, divorce, or absence due to work can account for parental absence, while infertility may result in the absence of children. In families with children, the absence of the mother was more disturbing than the absence of the father, while the absence of children stripped the mother of contact with people and institutions outside the home. It is interesting that 'if the role of each person is defined by the relation of father to mother to children, then the absence of one of those elements could be calamitous'.[30] There is no doubt that this patriarchal design taught. Much of its teaching, however, would be considered inadequate today, if not miseducative. It is not a design directed towards adulthood for all.

The patriarchal design of family was exposed and challenged by the feminist movement whose contribution has been to question the social and historical construction of the family. Indeed, feminists thinkers 'have challenged the assumption that the modern husband and full-time wife and mother, is the only legitimate family form to be aspired to in all times and places, either for biological or socio-functional reasons.'[31]

Such an assumption not only perpetuates male dominance of women and children, resulting in the uneven distribution of wealth and power, but serves to ignore other familial forms that have been in existence since time began.

Envisioning a transformed social order, the feminist perspective has the potential to open up the patriarchal form of family to other possibilities of communal life, allowing the universal value of community to be uncovered and embodied in the life of the family. In unravelling the threads of the old social order, a new tapestry is rewoven and a new picture emerges. New thought patterns and practices are conceived and come to birth in the redefinition of family life. Now the established familial relationships have been unmasked and new educative directions for the family's social form have been pointed out.

In urging the family to embody an alternative form of relationship, the feminist movement recognises how its teaching style is transformed. In this regard, it calls upon family members to reflect critically on their lives and on the ways in which they interact with one another. The purpose of such a reflection is not only to nullify existing patriarchal patterns, but also to capture the essence of what it means to be human. The identity of each family member is reshaped and a new form of human interaction is born. Now the family is the locus of a new structure of care, meaning and significance creating the environment in which people can grow towards psychological, social and religious maturity. The family now experiences a new way of life and teaches in a way that is more educative than miseducative. All family members show all family members how to live and how to die on their journey towards adulthood.

Teaching by Modelling/Performance
The reshaped family teaches in a way that differs from the patriarchal form of family.

Life is now patterned in a different way. The father is no longer head of the household. Power is shared equally between father and mother and the children share in this power commensurate with their stages in life. Each family member listens to and is responsive to each family member. The sexual life is no longer controlled by the male, but is expressed as a form of communication between mother and father. The father no longer has the sole responsibility for providing income and sustenance for the family. Rather, this occurs primarily through the collaboration of husband and wife, but also with each family member. The mother is no longer fully occupied with the children and the housework. These roles are now equally shared. The absence of a family member is less calamitous than was experienced in the pyramidic model of family life. In addition, since the mother is likely to be employed in the workforce as well as the father, the absence of children does not separate her from contact with people and institutions outside of the home.

In a word, it can be said that sex, power and work are now equally shared between husband and wife, and conversation within the family occurs in a more inclusive manner. Through the modelling of their mother and father and the manner in which they are invited to participate in family life, children learn the meaning of equality, respect, responsibility, discipline and justice. The pattern of family life now teaches mutuality, collaboration and inter-dependence. All this is illustrative of the fact that parents teach their children through modelling. The manner in which they speak and use words, together with the attitudes displayed through their actions, teach children life-long lessons of what it means to live in a family and in a community. The family here teaches by modelling and performing this way of being in the world.

However, the emancipatory changes that take place in the structure and design of family life do not occur in isolation, but in relation to other non-familial organisations with which the family has contact. Some of these include other families, neighbourhood groups, clubs, and voluntary associations, to name but a few.

The co-existence of familial and non-familial forms of community operates from the assumption that the words *family* and *community* can be clearly distinguished. According to Moran, this distinction seems obvious: 'family refers to the unit of parents and children; community means a personal grouping based on some shared values.'[32] The reality is, however, that in Western society, family is inclined to take over the meaning of community, while the word 'community' has been extended to embrace countless numbers of groups and systems. Despite these flaws, the word *community* refers to the communion that takes place between human persons and, therefore, its most obvious expression is found in the family. This new model of family/community does acknowledge family as a central expression of community, but recognises that it is only one expression and that other forms of intimacy and socialisation are necessary. The family, therefore, requires a framework of non-familial, but communal, forms of life. This relationship of family to other communal forms of life can be a profound modelling pedagogy.

Teaching languages within the family
The balanced mixture of teaching languages found within the family grace family members with an unusual richness. While all three families of languages are found in day-to-day familial life, the homiletic and therapeutic linguistic families have more prominence than that of academic discourse. Arising from a community existence, the first family of languages – storytelling, lecturing and preaching – manifests itself in family education. Beginning at birth, storytelling immerses the child in his or her familial, national, religious and mythological heritage, enabling the child to tap into the memory of the family and of the community. Little or no explanation is needed; the child is taught in the telling of the story. Stories have formative power and invite the child to express hopes, fears and dreams. Their power lies in their ability to shape lives.

Story-telling, as a teaching tool, is not reserved for children. Much of life consists of storytelling. For example, storytelling for older children and adults manifests itself in the form of gossip, joke-telling, novel reading and the watching of soap operas. The teachings of august philosophers and teachers are passed on in the form of stories. With contemporary developments in the computer and film industries, stories have the power to shape family and culture in ways previously unknown to humankind.

The first family of languages comprises two other languages, both of which are needed to complement storytelling. While lecturing and preaching may be intermittently found in family life, they do manifest themselves from time to time. For example, a seven-year old may need to be corrected for a misdemeanor and may be at the receiving end of words that parents hope will change his or her actions. Similarly, the heart of a sixteen-year-old adolescent may be stirred through the inspiring words of a parent who shares a meaningful aspect of his or her life. It is important to note, however, that the languages of lecturing and preaching are not confined to the parent-child relationship, but extend to the relationship between spouses, as well as that of siblings. In all circumstances the teaching involved appeals to the understanding of the listener.

The therapeutic set of teaching languages also finds prominence in the family setting. These are the languages 'that calm, soothe and heal', languages that are central to human life and, therefore, should be central to teaching.[33] The need for the therapeutic arises when family members experience brokenness in one form or another. When this occurs, people experience some form of disconnectedness and desire to be restored to the family community. What they need is speech that calms and soothes, speech in which they can experience welcome and thanks, confession and forgiveness, mourning and comfort. Mutuality is the essence of these therapeutic languages and within the family setting people experience them as a constant giving and receiving.

According to Moran, people within the family setting can be taught by *welcome/thank* to adopt a receptive attitude towards the universe and life and all that they entail. Thanking is a natural correlative to welcome. The teaching language of *confess/forgive* encourages a person to acknowledge the rupture that has occurred in family life and the experience of forgiveness enables the family to be recreated. The final pair of therapeutic languages, *mourn/comfort*, while explicitly related to dying, also pertains to the small *deaths* experienced in the family setting when one has to let go of something that is deeply valued. As family members grow older, they are continually being invited to let go of the stage they have outgrown, a process that can be painful in many circumstances. In a similar fashion, the circumstances of life demand that people let go of dreams, aspirations, hopes and desires, causing death-like experiences for many. The comfort, love and support of family members enables a person to deal with this experience and, hopefully, accept the invitation to new life.

The third teaching language, academic discourse, entails teaching the conversation. While teaching within the family is always a form of conversation, this family of languages is more suited to the classroom. However, it does take place in family life when the conversation concerns speech about speech. It occurs when parents help children with their homework and when children raise academic issues at the dinner table. It further occurs when spouses discuss the literature they have been reading, or when any form of academic discourse becomes the focal point of conversation. Dramatic performance takes place within the family when children are invited to perform for guests. Dialectical discussion can find prominence in family discussions when members seek a more reflective use of language and seek the meaning of words used in dialogue.

The family then teaches by modelling a way of life, and the languages of the homiletic and the therapeutic are at the centre of its linguistic daily life.

3. The Family as Moral Educator

The crucial role played by the family in the moral education of its members deserves highlighting. In the familial setting morality is taught on a daily basis through the manner in which family members interact. This lesson differs in accordance with the age of the recipient. For example, the moral lesson learned by a two-year old child varies from that learned by an older sibling, or by a thirty-five-year-old parent, or by a seventy-year-old grandparent. For the very young child, daily routine is the chief teacher of morality within the family, a factor that profoundly influences the child's moral future. In this way, the family provides the basis of both good and evil in the child's life, thereby illustrating that the family is the first and primary moral educator. This is also in keeping with traditional Roman Catholic teaching.

Moral education for the child begins from the first moments of life and is manifested in the ways in which he or she experiences care and nurture. From these early moments, the child imbibes the way of life he or she is shown. 'Children are taught by what they see, hear, touch and taste.'[34] To show love and care for a child teaches love and care. Unfortunately, some ways in which a child is taught morality can be miseducative. This can be seen when the child experiences abuse. If a child experiences physical or sexual abuse, that child is being taught a destructive lesson in violence.

Research and theory, however, have indicated that the family experiences limitations in the area of moral development. Durkheim, for example, believed that the school, not the family, was the primary moral educator of young people.[35] Bronfenbrenner, on the other hand, felt that the peer group was more influential than the family in moral matters, a situation he did not regard as beneficial. The positive and negative research findings concerning the family as moral educator, suggest that one must avoid the temptation of idealising the family as solely determining the moral development of its young and, on the other hand, rejecting the significant influence family can have on moral development. The genesis of moral development is certainly in the family, but it does continue outside the home.

Psychological theory and research have yielded important contributions in their attempts to clarify how values develop in the young. Behaviourism, for example, believes this occurs through *reinforcement* where right actions are praised and wrong actions are punished. Moral learning here is equated with moral behavior. Psychoanalytic theory, on the other hand, proposes that moral development takes place through *identification* and *internalisation,* a process in which children identify with and internalise parental wishes in order to avoid uncomfortable guilt feelings. *Modelling* is the process through which social learning theorists believe moral development takes place. Adopting the moral standards of a model, children develop styles of thinking, reasoning and judging. What the foregoing theories have in common is their belief that the role of the family in moral education is important but limited. This is a belief supported by the Christian tradition and illustrated through the writing of Robert N. Bellah.

Acknowledging the family as a basic unit in both social and spiritual life, Robert N. Bellah poses two pertinent questions with regard to the family as moral educator:

> How can we transmit to (children) a sense of moral responsibility and a religious understanding of life? How can we create within the family a moral and religious atmosphere than can withstand the pressures of the larger world in which we live?[36]

In attempting to answer these questions, Bellah believes that the family is too small and vulnerable to sustain the moral life of its members without any assistance and, therefore, needs the help of larger social structures. In this regard, he chooses the Church as a particular context for family life, but also includes the school, neighbourhood and the larger public realm as other means of support.

Family can have a formative influence on the lives of its members through the creation of a common culture, a culture with shared symbols and practices. Ritual is central to the idea of common culture and can be manifested through the common meal, recreation times, and holidays. The common meal, for example, invites all family members to share in its preparation, enjoyment and cleaning up. Sitting at table together provides the opportunity for children to learn how to interact in a respectful manner. 'The dinner table is', according to Bellah, 'a place to learn the rules of civil discourse and I can assure you that if they are not learned there, they are not likely to be learned in school.'[37] He also stresses that if what is learned in religious education classes is not reflected in family life it will not be retained. The common culture of family life, therefore, is crucial to moral education and the formation of character.

An example of family and Church working together in the moral education of the individual is depicted by Tom Inglis in his book *Moral Monopoly*. He sketches the role of the Irish mother in the moral monopoly of her husband and children. The role of moral education for the Irish mother began after the Famine when parliamentary commissions indicated that the transformation of Irish women into good mothers would have a civilising effect on Irish society. The task of good mothers was defined largely by priests and nuns and began with the priest gaining control of the woman's sexual life. In this regard, because of the woman's isolation in the home, she had no choice but to yield to the control of the priest and ally herself with the Church. 'For women to attain and maintain moral power', Inglis writes, 'it was necessary that they retain their virtue and chastity.'[38] The message that mothers passed onto their daughters was that moral responsibility entailed chastity and modesty. From the mid-1800s, therefore, the Irish mother became the central link between the Church and the individual, carrying the post-Famine moral code from the church and school to the home. Introducing changes in the Irish lifestyle, the Irish mother became the enforcer of moral discipline, a power she obtained and maintained through the Church. Relying heavily on support from the priest, as well as Church teaching, she was able to rule morally over her spouse and offspring. In so doing, the priest became her ally in her attempts to limit the words and actions of her husband. The result was that the perspective of the Irish mother became similar to that of the priests and religious and the children became indoctrinated into the rules and regulations of the Church.

Virtue and care, character and community
Questioning whether morality is a succession of reasonable judgments, or the formation of good character, Gabriel Moran explores the language of virtue and care, believing that '*virtue* including *care* will lead us back to *character* in *community*.'[39] Coming from the Latin translation of a Greek word, the etymological meaning of *virtue* is 'strength' or 'excellence'. Virtue directs the individual's ability to choose and is, according to Paul Philibert an 'assured capacity to call up practiced understanding.'[40] Virtue is acquired through a repetition inclusive of understanding and the virtuous person is one who has integrated his or her strengths.

In the philosophy of the ancient Greeks, as well as in the history of Christianity, morality was not diluted to behaviour or to the making of decisions. Rather, Plato, Aristotle and Aquinas believed that the person of morally good character made morally good decisions. For them, moral character was formed through participation in the 'life, story and vision of moral communities.'[41] Taking over the main virtues of these august philosophers and teachers, Christianity placed the virtues in a framework of 'unique persons, creativity and historical process' and morality came to be understood as a person's response to God the creator.[42]

The acquisition of virtues in an orderly fashion does not give a person a virtuous character. Character, rather, develops from a person's response to his or her physical and social environment and to the manner in which one responds to one's self-image, to the needs of others and to one's sense of wholeness. The family provides the groundwork for moral development by providing a family/community narrative. In doing this, it furnishes a story enabling members to know the story that is theirs and of which they are a part. In addition, the family educates members to value what is held in common and to embrace codes of behaviour, manners of address and ways of being together, particularly in the sharing of celebration, disappointment, hope and sorrow. As moral educator, the family enables its members to respond to the present moment in a faithful and careful way. Encouraging people to recognise the other person as gift, as a unique creation, the family becomes a place where understanding is deepened and imagination expanded.

The family teaches the ethic of virtue/care/character/community primarily through inspiration and imitation. Family members imbibe the attitudes and behaviours expected of them and become moral people by sharing in the life of a moral family. In this situation, it is not just the parents who educate morally. Each family member educates each family member toward moral character. At any given time a member may assume the role of teacher on any issue. Indeed, according to Moran, 'some of the most important aspects of moral development and moral education occur in infancy with the care the child receives and in childhood with games, stories, image formation and language.'[43] As an adult, the moral person is open to learning, aware that moral development continues until one draws his or her last breath.

The family as educator, teacher and moral educator
The family as educator, teacher and moral educator culminates in the family's form of life that directs and forms its members towards adulthood. In this regard, the formative process of family is oriented towards psychological, social and religious maturity, that is, towards the 'Kingdom of God'. This ideal of adulthood is marked by the synthesis or integration of opposites such as rational/non-rational, dependence/independence, life/death.[44] Adulthood comprises a combination of these characteristics, with adults possessing the ability to be 'serious *and* playful, artistic *and* logical'.[45] Combining dependence and independence, adults are able to be *interdependent* – with other human persons, nonhuman animals, and with the elements of the earth. This model of adulthood finds a home in the model of family where relationships within the family become mutual, cooperative and interdependent. In this way, all family members educate all family members towards the full expression of adulthood.

It is important to note, however, that the family, in educating its members towards adulthood, does not work in isolation. In fact, education towards adulthood will not be effective if it fails to engage the major institutions of society. This inter-institutional education has been described as 'a geographical interplay of human organisation.'[46] Education towards adulthood is a lifelong task and it is in working with these institutions that the integration of opposites may take place. The result is that the family, in supporting this ideal of adulthood, breaks free from the chains that segregate educational forms by age. Now everyone at every age can be educated towards adulthood by family, school, work and leisure. Now family members can work together towards psychological, social and religious maturity.

Conclusion

This chapter has illustrated the crucial role that the family plays in the religious education of all its members. In order to do this, it is important for the family to exercise its primary function as educator and teacher. The family educates, first and foremost, by being a family and by being a community. It teaches by design and by modelling a way of life, as well as through its engagement in the teaching languages. It also educates morally through demonstrating a way of life. To this end, the family accompanies its members towards psychological, social and religious maturity by showing them how to live and how to die. In other words, as educator, teacher and moral educator, the family accompanies each family member on the journey towards the 'Kingdom of God'.

Chapter 5

THE SCHOOL AS RELIGIOUS EDUCATOR

The second form of life within an educational framework concerns schooling. Here it is important to note the distinction between *schooling* as a form of education and *school* as a place of education. *Schooling* as a form is a lifelong phenomenon whereas *school* as a place is concerned with time, space and materials. For the purposes of this chapter, I will focus on school as a *place* of education.

The school is commonly understood as existing within the world of unreality. Gabriel Moran disputes this invalid perception and describes school as a place to retreat from the many cumbersome concerns of life. 'A school is a distinct location', he believes, 'where people step back from ordinary concerns to concentrate upon learning something.'[1] With this understanding, the classroom becomes one of the few available places concerned about the entire real world. It is, in the words of Theodore Sizer 'the real world found inside the school.'[2] In this sense, school would be better described as an extraordinary world rather than an unreal world. While almost any kind of learning can take place under the school roof, two distinct forms have dominated through the centuries: scientific or philosophical learning and task-oriented learning. Either or both forms of learning may be found in the modern school.

The school as religious educator engages in many forms of learning. In this chapter, I propose to examine the school under the headings of *school as educator, school as teacher* and *school as moral educator.* Aware that education today is more closely associated with school than it was a few centuries ago, an examination of the *school as educator* necessitates an exploration of the meaning of education. Contemporary educational language is challenged when differentiations are made between *school* and *schooling.* The social form of schooling towards knowledge is explored and special attention is paid to the unique manner in which school educates. The *school as teacher* theme explores the meaning of the verb *to teach* and notes the two forms of learning located in the school – classroom learning and learning outside of the classroom. The language of academic discourse, which specifically pertains to classroom teaching, is also explored. The theme of *school as moral* educator focuses on the close relationship that exists between the lifelong processes of moral education and religious education. Acknowledgement of this relationship facilitates the discussions of teaching morally and teaching morality (ethics) within the classroom. To these themes we now proceed.

1. The School as Educator

The meaning of education
While numerous books have been written on education, both the aim and nature of education, as noted earlier, remain a nebulous affair. In this regard, the most important question one can postulate regarding education is to enquire about its meaning. The meaning of the word *education* changed dramatically toward the end of the nineteenth century when it became closely associated with the school. Prior to this, education had a broader meaning, one that included both the human and nonhuman world. There were definite forms of education in existence besides the school and all were used by

society to transmit valuable learning from one generation to the next.

The drastic change in the meaning of education took place during the nineteenth century's Industrial Revolution. According to R. S. Peters, two developments contributed to this change. (1) The 'educated man' became the ideal of education. (2) Knowledge became the essential value in education.[3] The latter point resulted in a split between liberal and vocational education.

The late 1960s ushered in a period of acute analysis of education. This period witnessed numerous educational experiments, many of which were short-lived. For example, the curriculum was expanded to include 'real-life problems'. According to Herbert Kliebard, 'one major function of life adjustment education was its emphasis on the indefinite expansion of the scope of the curriculum.'[4] While some changes were advantageous, they continued to embody the underlying suppositions of current educational thought. In other words, the basic language with which to ask educational questions never changed. This could be due to the fact that when reformers become aware that education is not a product obtained in school, the question of an alternative meaning becomes rather threatening.

One thing that has become clear regarding the meaning of education is that it is not synonymous with what happens in schools. In order to break away from this mindset, Gabriel Moran suggests that the above discoveries by Peters might be beneficial today, not in the sense of returning to an earlier era, but in the sense of restoring their context.[5] In this regard, he suggests that the 'educated man' be placed in the context of women, animals and plants so that people are educated with the full awareness of ecology. Secondly, he calls for both academic and manual learning for everybody. This leads him to describe an alternate model of education that comprises a 'finite set of interacting forms.'[6] In observing how and where people learn, he identified four areas of learning shared by most people: family life, schooling, work and retirement. The problem, as we know, is that these forms tend to be age-segregated. The family form of learning is thought to be for very young children, the school for those aged between five and eighteen years, work for the adult, and retirement for the elderly. Education, however, is lifelong and takes place through the interplay of all four forms.

Lawrence A. Cremin also recognises the need for a new relationship between two contrasting worlds of education – the classroom and society at large.[7] He acknowledges the educational activities that occur in the multiplicity of institutions punctuating contemporary society. In his thought, the ways in which these institutions relate to, and engage, one another point to the configurations of education permeating our modern world. Taking Dewey's distinction between *schooling* and *education*, Cremin develops the idea of intentional education. In this regard, he indicates that it occurs in the family, workplace and church, as well as through the medium of books, television and the arts.

Discussing the limitations of progressive educational theory, Cremin criticises John Dewey for focusing 'so exclusively on the potentialities of the school as a lever of the social improvement and reform as to ignore the possibilities of other educative institutions.'[8] In his view, Dewey went awry when he discussed *incidental* versus *intentional* education and focused more on the origins of institutions than on their functions. Cremin's argument, on the other hand, strives to illustrate the educative role of family life, religious life and organised work.

In proposing an ecological approach to education, Cremin's thesis is latitudinarian in that he indicates the range of variety of institutions that educate people in the course of their lives. In this regard, he suggests that education be thought of comprehensively, relationally and publicly. It must be comprehensive in that consideration must be given to all the situations and institutions in which education occurs. It must be relational in its awareness of past and present activities going on elsewhere. Finally, it must be public in that education becomes a great big public debate. To this end, Cremin maintains:

> The questions we need to ask about education are among the most important questions that can be raised in our society, particularly at this juncture in its history. What knowledge should 'we the people' hold in common? What values? What skills? What sensibilities? When we ask such questions, we are getting to the heart of the kind of society we want to live in and the kind of society we want our children to live in. We are getting to the heart of the kind of public we would like to bring into being and the qualities we would like that public to display. We are getting to the heart of the kind of community we need for our many individuals to flourish.[9]

The social form of schooling/knowledge

Schooling is an experience pertinent to education and is a major way in which human knowledge can be arranged and absorbed. As an educational experience, it is a partial embodiment of the universal value of knowledge. Knowledge, in this context, refers to the ability of the human person to grasp world events. It can refer to the storing of information or to the acquisition of wisdom. In this regard, it is beneficial to distinguish between *schooling* as a form of education and *school* as the usual venue in which learning takes place. Schooling can be regarded as 'less than school (as something that occurs in the school building along with lunch, breaks, and extra-curricular activities) and something larger than the school (i.e. a system involving teacher unions, country administrators and publishers)'.[10] Therefore, it pertains to a specific form of life and learning.

School educates in a unique manner by placing a strong emphasis on academic learning. Highlighting the value of literate knowledge, learning in school is conveyed through books, classrooms and schoolteachers. Its concern lies with speaking, reading and writing. Making language accessible to people, schooling as a form of education has the ability to exercise the imagination and provide people with the facility to progress well in life.

As a form of learning, schooling suggests a definite collection of materials, intentions and results. It pertains to a form in which space, time, materials and people are intentionally used to impart knowledge and skills. The *space* for schooling is any venue where activity is directed toward learning. The usual place for this is the school. Requiring a long period of *time*, schooling takes up a substantial part of each day or week and may last for years. Books and related materials form the *materials* of school, while the *persons* involved in school are the schoolteachers. Although schooling is a unique form of education, 'it cannot always be breathlessly exciting, personally relevant and socially constructive.'[11] Eva Brann is in agreement when she writes that 'the daily life of even the best of schools must be a mundane mastering of other people's reflection.'[12]

In describing the manner in which the school educates, it is important not to assume that the learners are aged between five and eighteen years. Most books pertaining to school operate from the assumption that a classroom is where older people give instruction to younger people. Not denying the classroom's special relation to the young, it is important to remember that it is not theirs exclusively. Indeed, certain aspects of classroom learning are reserved for older people, those who can engage in abstract and critical thinking.

Schooling begins at birth and continues until the moment of death. Therefore, schooling is for people of all ages – infants, young children, older children, adolescents, young adults, middle-aged adults and the elderly. 'Schooling', Moran writes, 'ought to be for everyone some of the time and for no one all of the time.'[13] Classroom learning, therefore, belongs to every age group.

In describing schooling as a form of education, Moran draws attention to the psychological tension existing between the two great moments of 'distance' and 'within'. Schooling, by its very nature, involves a dispassionate examination of the fruits of the world's great thinkers. Therefore, it requires a *distancing* of oneself from external personal involvements. It also, however, begins from *within* the personal experience of the learner. The learner begins from within his or her own interests, suppositions and biases. How, therefore, can one's experience from within be related to one's ability to distance oneself as a thinker? The answer lies in schooling. 'Schooling is a moment for the emphasis of distancing though never to the complete exclusion of experience from within.'[14]

In summary, then, it can be said that schooling educates in a unique manner. It educates by providing literacy and academic instruction, by introducing the mind of the learner to the great thinkers of the world and by facilitating the marriage between distancing oneself with experience from within.

2. The School as Teacher

Classroom teaching is one of the four major forms of lifelong and lifewide education and is related to other forms of teaching, both inside and outside the school. Recognising that this act is central to teaching, it is helpful to approach the issue of school by questioning the meaning of *to teach*. Although teaching is not the whole of education, it does provide an important test case of how education is understood. John Dewey, for example, on the rare occasions when he used the verb *to teach*, understood it as a task executed by schoolteachers (*educators*).[15] Education, he assumed, was something children received in a classroom. Many educational writers operate from a similar assumption, that teaching involves powerful people telling powerless people what to think. This is a factor that subverts the relation between teacher and student.

The act of teaching, as noted earlier, can best be described by the etymology of the verb *to teach*: to teach is to show how. To teach, therefore, means showing someone how to do something, an act executed by every human being. This act of showing how can be done in many ways and in many settings. Such an understanding of teaching has no fundamental connection to children or, indeed, to any specific age. An appreciation of teaching as an exchange that takes place between adults would remove the assumption that it is something adults do to children and, at the same time, enable the involvement of children in a more sensitive way. A good test of any pedagogical theory is whether it can be applied to the most vulnerable in society – the very young, the very old and those with special needs. The inclusion of these vulnerable groups would illustrate that showing someone how to do something is, for the most part, a nonverbal activity. The showing is done predominantly through gestures and symbols.

The nonverbal aspect of teaching regards the teacher as possessing *know-how*, someone who knows how to pass knowledge onto somebody else. Evidence of this can be found in the teaching of a child to ride a bicycle, to tie shoe laces, to play a sport or a musical instrument. All of these instances are concerned with movement of the body, an obvious starting point for any reflection on the meaning of teaching. It is important that schoolteachers are mindful of this fact and recognise that their concern has more to do with words. While language acquisition occurs within the first years of life, the role of the schoolteacher is to enable the child to become reflectively self-conscious, with the power to abstract language from things. This does not happen all at once, but takes place through the child's conceptual development. 'The strange thing is that our society seems to believe that schoolteaching should stop just when the power to school-learn is finally acquired.'[16]

The above situation leads to the suspicion that schools are not as concerned with teaching as one might think. For example, is the full acquisition of verbal and conceptual skills the primary concern of schools? The history of schoolteaching in the nineteenth and twentieth centuries points to the fact that primary and secondary schools are absorbed with nurture. Teaching was regarded as the natural extension of womanhood. According to Sheila Rothman 'the education necessary to fit a woman to be a teacher, is exactly the one that best fits her for that domestic relation she is primarily designed to fill.'[17] The university, on the other hand, is concerned with lecturing. This is an activity, carried out predominantly by men who, preferring not to be perceived as nurturers, engage in a mixture of lecturing, preaching and discussion. However, the task of the schoolteacher or university professor is not to nurture or to lecture, but 'to show how to use words and concepts to understand this world.'[18]

Teaching may be described as a bodily activity, an activity embodied in the life of the community. In many forms of teaching, speech functions as choreography. This is evident when someone is learning how to dance, drive, cook or swim. Specific directions are received and given through human speech and written texts. Teaching is concerned with reshaping movement, and language is perceived to be a human movement. The movement of language within the act of teaching, as we noted earlier, takes three forms: homiletic, therapeutic and academic discourse. While each of these languages has an important contribution to make, each has the potential to weaken the entire radius of teaching when it perceives itself as being the only way to teach. The form most appropriate to classroom teaching is academic discourse.

Academic discourse

Central to academic discourse are dialectical discussion and academic criticism, both of which draw their content from the other two families of languages. Academic discourse, however, is not confined to school, but is present in many books and discussions. Indeed, 'academic speech requires a stringent set of conditions that may be difficult to establish outside the school.'[19]

While the homiletic and therapeutic languages of teaching have a legitimate place in school, their immediate contexts are external activity and inner healing respectively. Academic speech, on the other hand, is concerned, almost totally, with speech. Here the nature and meaning of particular texts are examined and speech is turned back on itself. Academic speech, therefore, is 'speech about speech.'[20]

Overlapping the homiletic and therapeutic, the academic language of teaching is more than a combination of these languages. It can be as directive as preaching or as nondirective as therapy, but its particularity lies in the word 'instruction', a word that Moran says 'calls us back to the body.'[21]

Used primarily for physical activities, the word *instruction*, preceded by the adjective *academic* signifies a precise and direct use of speech. Academic instruction, therefore, bends speech back on speech, a factor that eliminates any authoritarian element. Rather than being told what to think, people are invited to examine their modes of speaking. Being neither interested nor uninterested speech, academic discourse can be described as disinterested speech in the sense that human beings can temporarily let go of their involvements and beliefs in order to examine suppositions, circumstances, and areas of personal myopia.

Forms of schoolteaching

School, as a location, may be divided into two main forms of learning – the classroom and the areas outside of the classroom. Before commenting on these two learning forms, it is important to recognise school itself as a form of teach-learn. School, because of its very existence, is a teacher. 'The community and the physical environment', Moran writes, 'are always teaching in a school.'[22] Whether the lessons they teach are good or bad, the fact is that they are powerful teachers.

Classroom teaching: While teaching may go on outside the classroom walls, specific attention must be paid to what goes on within the hallowed walls of that environment. Indeed, there are certain conditions necessary for this strangest form of teaching-learning to take place. Aware that the spoken word is the clear focus of the classroom, the physical setting of that room must instill a sense of quietness and be dedicated more to the ear than the eye. Some suggestions include an adequate supply of fresh air, ample lighting and the least amount of disturbance from external sources. Thought-provoking discussion is facilitated by the presence of carpeting and movable chairs, which make the room more comfortable. If a platform exists, it is for students as well as teachers, particularly when students engage in the teaching activity. The presence of technology, including a chalkboard must not create a clutter in the classroom. Rather, its purpose is to envelop the primary area where conversation takes place. The spoken word is the main activity of the classroom. According to Ernest Boyer, the classroom is one of the few places available where people might listen carefully to the voice of another and change their minds.[23]

Although the classroom is frequently accused of being more concerned with talk than action, an understanding of action as verbal or nonverbal can illustrate how verbal action within the classroom can change the world. Educational reformers through the ages have begun with the premise of *learn by doing*. While this principle is central to teaching, it must never be forgotten that speech is the action of the classroom. To place other actions into the classroom is, according to Moran, to 'obscure the *kinds of speech* appropriate for the classroom.'[24] It is for this reason that the third family of languages comprising dramatic performance, dialectical discussions and academic criticism, holds a special place in the classroom. 'The classroom', Moran writes, 'is a dialogue about dialogue, a reflecting upon the preconditions of conversation, the ambiguities of any genuine human speech, the possibilities of organizing large bodies of information.'[25] It provides an entry point from which learners can begin to converse with the human race.

Dramatic performance involves playing with language. The unfolding drama may reveal the presence of a story. The story, in this instance, is not the vehicle of teaching. That is reserved for the teaching language of storytelling in the homiletic family of languages. Rather, dramatic performance places a distance between the speaker and the story. This can best be manifested in the form of role playing where learners are invited to reflect on the words they use. The role playing of a volatile issue, for example, can alter the perspective of the entire gathering.

Dialectical discussion forms the second language in this third family of languages. Differing from the types of discussion that occur in the workplace or canteen, dialectical discussion finds structure in the classroom. This type of discussion entails going back and forth in an effort to get closer to the truth. In this regard, it is a discussion that never ends. In the classroom setting, the schoolteacher leads people to and places them in the centre of the conversation of the human race. The conversation begins when learners encounter the mind of a great thinker. It finds embodiment in the human conversation that takes place in the classroom.

The third language in the family of teaching the conversation is *academic criticism*, the language particularly intended for the classroom. In the previous two languages of dramatic performance and dialectical discussion, the questioning centred on the meaning of the words. Now, the very meaning of the words themselves is the question. In using the interrogative, academic criticism postulates Who?, Why?, What? It asks questions such 'As according to whom?', 'Why?', 'What are the presumptions and implications?' The posing of serious questions in this way enables the learner's questions to be released and gives him or her the chance to become a teacher. All this reveals that the word is central to classroom teaching.

Performance areas: In the previous section, we encountered the classroom as a single area within the school. Now we turn to performance areas as the second main form of school learning. These areas are, of necessity, plural. Comprising mainly art, job-related work and sports, the performance areas appropriately complement the verbal instruction of classroom teaching.

Education in the arts is essential to the lifelong education of each person. While education in the aesthetics can begin before five years of age and continue until death, it is important that schools designate spaces for laboratory, studio or concert hall in order to furnish students with some artistic experience. Many of the verbal arts are linked to classroom teaching. Examples of these include a class or school play, debating and learning to speak a language. Other arts are less verbal in nature and comprise, for example, learning to drive, learning to play a musical instrument or learning a sport. Participation in some of these arts teaches students the meaning of silence and discipline. Others teach the value of teamwork.

A second performance area concerns job performance. Classroom teaching is complemented by the performance of skills that would benefit a student in a current or future job. The task of the school here is not principally to begin work programs, but to improve the relationship between various forms of learning in existence. Where it is not possible to provide students with realistic experiences of the job world within the school walls, the school must look to outside sources. In addition, the schoolteacher has to question how the academic learning in the classroom may be regarded as real work and how it can contribute toward job satisfaction now and in the future.

Sports provide a third performance area in the school. The teaching-learning activity involved in sports teaches people powerful lessons concerning life and death. People who participate in sports frequently learn about discipline, motivation, and the importance of working as a team. This is a performance area that would be beneficial for each member of the school community.

Teaching religion in schools
Teaching religion in schools is an important aspect of schooling in religious education. Teaching religion in a classroom is an academic process. It is not concerned with initiating people in religious matters. Neither is it preoccupied with teaching a person a religious way of behaving. Rather, the question involves what it means 'to show a person how to use words and concepts so as to understand a field called religion.'[26] In this regard, it is no different from the teaching of any other subject such as geography, history, science or mathematics.

Teaching religion in a classroom involves, first and foremost, presenting the material in an intelligible manner. The actions and verbal expressions of religious people can be proffered in a way that makes sense. However, this must be done with an air of caution. While it may be impossible to make sense of some contemporary religious movements, one must not draw any final conclusions about the more ancient religious traditions. All a teacher can do is present the language of a religious tradition in such a way that it is partially comprehensible. This is because of the peculiar character of religious language, a character that renders its meaning intelligible only up to a certain point. Moran explains why. 'Religious systems do not claim to explain the world completely, but they do claim to give a more comprehensive meaning to experience than any other systems.'[27]

Religious texts can only be understood when they are approached with openness, compassion and respect. When this occurs, the appropriate framework is created in which the text is enabled to act as mediator between the past and present. The task of the schoolteacher is to make sure that the text has the opportunity to realise its goal. Philip Phenix describes this task as a form of 'disciplined intersubjectivity.'[28] By this he means that the insights of a community are shared with another community through the medium of symbols. The schoolteacher, therefore, has to be exceedingly fair and disciplined in discerning the meaning of what was written in the context of another age. 'The chief criteria of this disciplined intersubjectivity', Moran writes, are fairness and fullness.'[29]

In order to understand the meaning of a religious text, it is necessary to take part in that meaning to a certain extent. The teacher must be able to view the world from the writer's perspective. In the school setting, teaching involves interpreting and reinterpreting, questioning and analysing the religious text. The result may be acceptance or it may entail rejection and resistance on the part of the learners. Whatever the outcome, the primary task of schoolteaching is to raise questions. In this regard, we can take comfort in the words of Rainer Maria Rilke:

> be patient towards all that is unsolved in your heart and try to love the questions themselves like locked rooms... Do not now seek the answers; that cannot be given you because you would not be able to live them. And the point is, to live everything. Live the questions now. Perhaps you will then gradually, without noticing it, live along some distant day into the answer.[30]

Any attempt to understand religion must begin with one's own religion. But to know the self we must have a sense of the other. This is because understanding entails comparing. In order to understand one's own religion, one must compare it to another religion, aware of the existence of many other perspectives. Moran identifies the issue of perspective as being central to any good classroom instruction. In this situation, the teacher always presents two perspectives to the learner: 'I stand behind the truth in what I am now saying, but it is also the case that my formulating of this truth is subject to improvement from other truths.'[31]

By way of summary, it can be said that schooling in religion, is an academic affair. Religion is the subject matter. The task is to teach it, like any other academic subject. This is an indispensable form of religious education.

3. The School as Moral Educator

Teaching morally
Both the meaning of *moral* and the meaning of *education* have too narrow a meaning in our modern understanding of moral education. The word *moral* followed by the word *education* has led to the widespread assumption that the task of moral education belongs to the school. On the other hand, people question whether it is possible to teach morality. The result is that endless confusion abounds in relation to the area of moral education.

Preceding the question regarding the possibility of teaching morality lies the concern of teaching morally. How does one teach morally? This question arises from the widespread suspicion that surrounds the act of teaching. Teaching, in the eyes of many people, is deemed to be an unethical act. It cannot be done morally. This problem is perfectly understandable if one uses the operative image of teaching that infiltrates some educational theories – that is, an adult telling a child what to do and think. Indeed, two unsavoury attitudes regarding teaching dominate this train of thought – the premise of inequality and the requirement of discipline. It is important to note, however, that while teaching begins with an unequal relationship between teacher and learner, its aim is to create equals. When one understands the verb *to teach* as showing someone how to do something, the fear that teaching is an immoral act is alleviated.

Gabriel Moran's way of addressing this problem has been to retreat from classroom teaching in order to explore the meaning of teaching in other situations. 'Unless these other kinds of teaching are taken seriously', he writes, 'schoolteachers will inevitably be asked to do more than is possible and other than what is ethically defensible.'[32] There is no moral conflict inherent in the fundamental meaning of *to teach* – showing someone how to do something.

A more complete perspective on teaching begins with acknowledging the special giftedness of teaching, a gift that evokes a personal response. Offering gifts on a daily basis, the entire universe may be regarded as the most extensive teacher. The human person can decide whether to accept or reject these gifts of learning and, therefore, the potential for moral conflict is not present in this situation. This potential occurs only with the introduction of the human community as teacher. The very essence of being human entails living in a teaching-learning relationship with the human community. Thus, the human person has no choice but to accept being taught.

The full emergence of a moral problem arises when an individual is given the title *teacher*. Now conditions under which one can legitimately teach must be examined. Times and places indicating an acceptance of the teaching-learning process must be set up, with the learner agreeing to one or more forms of learning. In this way, the moral authority of the teacher will be evident and students will learn through co-operation. Although the teaching-learning process is never exempt from the possibility of corruption, evidence to the contrary illustrates that teaching is a morally good activity.

The task of educating morally is not confined to one life form. 'An educational morality has to include all the forms of life that educate.'[33] Beginning in the family and continuing throughout schooling, work and retirement, moral education is carried out by people who move from one kind of teaching form to another without conscious reflection. To the extent that each form is appropriate, these people are teaching morally.

Teaching, Moran believes, is moral when it is 'responsible, trans-natural and private/public.'[34] Moral teaching is *responsible* when it responds to the situation. Postulating why these people are gathered here, the morally responsible teacher must not ignore the relational context within which he or she is showing someone how to do something. It means respecting the learner and being attentive to responses. It is *trans-natural* when it does not oppose nature, but goes beyond it, thereby contributing to a 'human transformation of the natural.'[35] Finally, teaching is *private/public* when it relates the 'private inner world and the large public world.'[36] No teacher has the right to intrude into the soul of another human being. It is the learner's prerogative whether he or she wants to learn. The teaching-learning process can only begin when the desire to learn comes from within the learner.

Teaching morally in schools

The moral life is taught by the school that has character and virtue. The school teaches morally primarily by example and by its way of behaving. In its total environment of space, arrangements and interrelations, the school teaches morally by modelling how one should live.

Within the school environment parents and schoolteachers, students and friends, secretarial and ancillary staff all teach morally on a daily basis. Most of the time this is not a conscious effort, but takes place unconsciously as people encounter what each moment brings.

The three teaching languages of preaching, therapy and instruction are present in the total life of the school. While the language of teaching the conversation is the language best suited to classroom instruction, the other two teaching languages of preaching and therapy are found in other parts of the school. Schools teach morally to the extent that the appropriate teaching language is used in the correct environment. For example, for the most part, the language of instruction does not belong to the chaplain or counsellor's room and the language of therapy does not belong to the classroom. In a word, teaching morally in schools concerns using the appropriate teaching language in the appropriate educational contexts.

Teaching morality

Regarding *how to teach morality*, Moran notes the remarkable similarity concerning the manner of teaching that exists within the diverse systems of the major world religions. The teacher, for example, is someone whose life and presence is an inspiration to others. Focusing on the daily lives of a few disciples, he or she provides moral guidance through example and preaching. Discipline emerges through 'community experience and the thousand daily rituals that weave the fabric of community relations: respect, care, compassion, courtesy, gratitude, patience.'[37] Morality is regarded as going beyond rules of behaviour and moral education is considered to be lifelong.

In exploring the issue of *what to teach in morality*, most of the world's religious traditions operate from the premise that 'what is unnatural is immoral.'[38] Inherent in this statement is a preservation of the world's goods. Any act of destruction is deemed to be immoral. 'A religious morality', Moran writes, 'is not based on a love of nature but on a care for natures, for each organism in its uniqueness.'[39]

Acknowledging school as the central community in the lives of children, Moran states that school 'in its total environment of physical space, temporal arrangements and human interaction is a main teacher of morality.'[40] Schools teach morality primarily by example. As a moral community, the school illustrates the practice of virtue. Within the school setting, morality is taught by other children and by the adult lives of all teachers and staff. The main indicator of what adults are teaching children derives from the interaction of adults with one another.

> ... schools are always acting morally or immorally. Every written and unwritten rule in the school implies an attitude toward the student's dignity and selfhood. How children line up for the bus, eat in the cafeteria, get permission to use the toilet, and get spoken to over the public address system have an effect on the student's (and the teacher's) moral sense.[41]

Teaching morality in classrooms
It is important to pay attention to two challenges raised by the teaching of morality in a classroom. What light does teaching *morality* in a classroom throw upon teaching anything in a classroom? How does the *classroom's* part in teaching morality relate to the teaching of educational settings.[42]

A few points are noteworthy in attempting to answer these questions. First, the title *morality* is inadequate for the teaching of morality as an academic form. Moran prefers to use the term *ethics*. Secondly, the objection of some people to the teaching of morality/ethics in a classroom raises questions about their assumptions concerning the meaning of *to teach*. Third, the classroom, as we have seen, is not a place where people are told the truth. Rather, it is a place that facilitates a peculiar form of conversation. It does not matter whether the student agrees with the teacher. What does matter is that the student has a better comprehension of the topic under discussion. The teaching of ethics, therefore, in a classroom situation 'is to show a student how to use a language of morality that can improve his or her understanding.'[43] It is to furnish the language in which people can reflect on the moral life in a clear, comprehensive and consistent way.

The points of view of the teacher of ethics must be twofold: the truth of the position drawn from the riches of human history and geography and, secondly, the openness to know that the position does not contain the whole truth, but is in need of further improvement. These points of view are not just confined to the ethics teacher but pertain to teachers of other academic subjects.

The essential point of the teaching of ethics is that it does not take place in isolation. It is imperative that it forms *part* of the rest of education in morality. The aim of education and, indeed moral education, is to improve the lives of all human beings, as well as relations between the human and nonhuman worlds. Within this framework, the role of teaching ethics in the classroom situation is to keep 'education in morality from becoming either neutral techniques or conformity to rules.'[44]

The School as Educator, Teacher and Moral Educator

The school as educator, teacher and moral educator has a specific contribution to make to the individual's journey towards adulthood. It does this, for example, through the manner in which the school environment is shaped. In this regard, the school has to choose between two alternatives – an authoritarian form of organisation in which people are segregated by age, sex and other factors, and a community-based education through which interdependence is promoted. The latter understanding of adulthood invites schools to provide a model of education that includes people of all ages. Teaching is no longer understood as giving explanations from the front of the classroom, but embodies its true essence of showing someone how to do something. In this way, people are encouraged to grow together towards psychological, social and religious maturity.

The school educates towards adulthood by paying attention to, and working with, other educative forms in existence (for example, the family, workplace, and times of leisure). In promoting the interplay of these life forms, the school can educate towards an adulthood that is mature, wise and integral.

As we have seen, the *design* of the school educates towards adulthood. Now it is important to focus attention on the manner in which the school *curriculum* educates towards adulthood. The two venues in which education towards adulthood takes place within the school setting are the performance or non-classroom areas and the classroom. In the performance areas, people are directed towards psychological, social and religious maturity through their participation in the arts, sports and music. Whether one plays a sport or a musical instrument, one is being educated towards maturity through the very act of participating. Through the arts, people are exposed to a whole range of experiences that contribute to the process of psychological, moral and religious maturity. For example, the need for practice teaches discipline and the value of solitude. It also teaches the meaning of teamwork and the effect of working together towards a unified goal. Most of all, participating in the performance areas educates towards adulthood, a maturity towards which people grow into all their lives.

Education towards adulthood also takes place in the classroom and occurs through schooling in the various subjects. In this regard, teaching the conversation in every subject matter, whether it is history, geography or religion, ought to lure and direct the students (young and old) towards a vision of psychological, social and religious maturity. The short-term goal in studying these subjects may be to succeed at examinations. The final analysis, however, is towards a goal without end, toward a point with no termination. The aim is to foster a mature person.

Conclusion

This chapter has examined the important contribution of schooling to religious education. It has shown how the essence of schooling involves educating and teaching. The school as educator examined the meaning of education and paid special attention to the social form of schooling/knowledge. In this regard, it examined the unique way in which schools educate. The school as teacher discussed the manner in which school teaches both in the classroom and in the performance areas. The teaching language of academic discourse was highlighted as being most suitable for the classroom. The school as moral educator explored the difference between teaching morally, teaching morality and teaching morality (ethics) in the classroom. From the discussion thus far, it can be seen that religious education, has the potential to enable people of every age and of every strata in society to become truly intelligently religious.

Chapter 6

THE PARISH AS
RELIGIOUS
EDUCATOR

We now take up the role of the parish or congregation as religious educator. Before dealing with this topic, it is important to situate the parish in relation to Gabriel Moran's educational framework. As was noted in previous chapters, his model of education comprises four social forms: family, schooling, work and leisure. Chapters Four and Five, respectively, discussed the educational roles of family and school. Chapter Six, in proposing to examine the educational form of the parish, explores the social forms of work and leisure as they are experienced within the parish setting. In this environment, work and leisure are intrinsically linked. People engage in work through their involvement in service to others, while service to others grows out of the prayer-life (leisure-time) of the congregation.

This chapter, therefore, proposes to examine the role of the parish as religious educator. This will be done through an examination of the parish under the themes of *parish as educator, parish as teacher* and *parish as moral educator*. Throughout these themes the richness of the ecclesiastical terms – *koinonia* (community), *leiturgia* (prayer), *didache* (teaching), *kerygma* (proclamation) and *diakonia* (service) will be interwoven. The theme of *parish as educator* will explore how the parish educates by design and by modelling. In this regard, it examines the parish as a religious body (community), as well as the manner in which the parish educates through modelling a life of prayer and service. The *parish or congregation as teacher* theme examines the meaning of teaching people to be religious. It does this by enquiring into the manner in which the parish engages the languages of teaching. In the theme of *parish as moral educator,* it will be seen that the parish educates morally by design and by example. Community is the design best suited to this endeavour. The parish also educates morally by modelling a way of life, especially by the example of service. Three specific ways in which this occurs includes teaching morally, teaching morality and teaching morality (ethics) in the classroom of the parish. To these themes we now proceed.

1. The Parish as Educator

There are two primary ways in which the parish fulfills its role as educator: 1) in educating by design and 2) in educating through modelling. Taking each in turn, this section begins by examining the way in which the parish educates by design. The word *design*, as we know, connotes a double meaning. Gabriel Moran explains. In educating by design, the parish educates by intention, for example, by being conscious of what is educating. Secondly, it educates through the design employed in transmitting its message. Any conscious attempt to educate, therefore, involves the imposition of design. In this regard, the parish, in its endeavor to educate, becomes aware that it is already working with and within a design. The best it can do, in its role as educator, is to improve upon the present design.

Educating by design

The educational design best suited to the parish setting is that of community. In order to understand more fully what is meant by this educative role, it is necessary to state what a community is, as well as to outline the characteristics of community. By community is meant something that is specifically human. Referring to human unity, the community contains implications that are positive and desirable. Gabriel Moran explains this further when he writes: 'A human unity means at the least that the human is not destroyed but that it is in some (perhaps unexpected) ways affirmed.'[1] In other words, since the actions of a community intend to promote the human, the question of morality is always present. A moral sense, therefore, is characteristic of the parish community.

As a human unity, community within the parish can be understood in two ways. First, it suggests the ideal of human unity to which one aspires. This understanding is at the heart of philosophical and religious quest. Secondly, it concerns the actual manifestation of that ideal in microcosmic form. 'A group which can legitimately appropriate the term community', Moran writes, 'has to demonstrate that the ideal universal community can be realised on the micro scale of the small group.'[2] Representing two sides of the same coin, these two meanings form a single relation. In other words, the parish community educates by partially embodying the ideal and by making it a reality in practice.

The human unity that characterises the parish community also points to the existence of diverse elements that need to be unified. Acknowledging the existence of 'the one and the many', the temptation might be to eradicate the many or else deny the presence of diversity. As an educating community, the role of the parish is to resist this tendency. Its task, rather, lies in embodying the diversity in unity of the entire human population.

Community is built upon the formation of mutual or reciprocal relations. The chief quality of the parish community, therefore, may be described as 'mutuality of relationship.'[3] All other characteristics of community are based on this fundamental human activity. There are degrees of mutuality, however, that are dependent upon the actual size of the community. For example, the degree of mutuality experienced in a large parish is very different from that encountered by a small parish. In order to be a practical and positive demonstration of what it means to live in community, it is recommended that the numbers be limited. In this regard, the purpose of the parish community is not to form an alternate social system, but, in Moran's words, to be 'an alternative component of the larger society.'[4] As a community, therefore, the parish educates by not attempting to solve all political problems. Rather, it educates by becoming one of the essential factors in coping with those issues, namely, being a genuine communal body.

It is important to remember, however, that in its role as educator, the purpose of the parish community is not to accomplish a task outside itself. Rather, its value lies in being a community. Its strength and significance are found in 'that organic kneading together of a personal life.'[5] This is the factor that sustains current members and attracts those who wish to join. People today seek community. They search for that which gives context and strength to their everyday lives. This search for community is highlighted by Oliver V. Brennan when, talking about young people, he writes that 'post-modern youth are involved in a threefold search: the experience of an intimate, non-uniform caring community; the experience of transcendence; and a sense of mission'[6]. In this regard, the parish educates through those rites and symbols that enable people to get in touch with who they are and where they come from. It enables them to be present, not only to themselves, but also to other persons and to the nonhuman world.

Living as a human community is not to suggest that the parish does not experience any difficulties. No community is perfect. Indeed, every community is affected by the de facto segregation contaminating the universe and to this end the parish as community is no exception. By this is meant that the parish community is afflicted with many of the divisions that cause oppression and destruction in the larger world. The test of the community's genuineness, however, is now apparent. It does not depend so much on whether the community has solved the problem but rather on whether 'it is working its way toward greater diversity in wholeness.'[7] If it does so, its communal life will be enriching and developmental – in other words, educational.

The religious meaning of community

By way of recapitulation, it has been said that community comprises a small number of people who express in specific form the diversity in unity of the entire human population. It has also been noted that each community is contaminated by some of the issues that cause division and segregation throughout the human race. Here, the adjective *religious* can be introduced to act as a counterforce to these divisions. A religious community, therefore, can be described as 'a group of people who, bound together in part by their religious heritage, refuse in principal to accept the de facto segregation.'[8] The religious meaning of community now becomes a more complete expression of what was heretofore experienced in community. The religious is a resistance *within* a communal life to closure and division. It is a protest (calling) for wholeness and unity.

The religious meaning of community is distinctly grounded in Jewish and Christian history where community is the locus of the religious. In the Judeo-Christian tradition, people have been called by God, not as individuals, but as a community. In a religious community, presence is heightened through rituals and symbols. It is out of life together as a people that forms of worship, teaching and service develop and make sense. Being present and being in community become synonymous. Presence is experienced as being in relationship with oneself, others and the non-human world. Its interest lies 'in responding to the possibilities of the present and retaining a sense of continuity over generations.'[9]

The ecclesiastical term for community is *koinonia*. Maria Harris proposes koinonia as 'the initial educational ministry' of the parish, the starting point for all curricular activity in the church.[10] Her writings re-echo the sentiments of Moran.

However, it is painfully obvious that community is not yet realised. Moran cites two examples.[11] The ability of the parish to educate by community is threatened by two factors: (1) the existence of the slogan *institutional Church*, a slogan that is more prevalent in Catholic than Protestant Churches, and (2) the presence of an authoritarian form of organisation. In terms of the first, the Church, by its very existence, is an institution and, therefore, the term *institutional Church* is a redundancy. While the particular institutional pattern produced by the Church needs correcting, the continued existence of the phrase *institutional Church* prevents the transformation of the Christian Church into a community that is genuinely religious.

The second factor concerns the pattern of power. The authoritarian form of organisation prevalent in the Christian Church throughout the ages finds its genesis in the belief that God revealed a message in the first century and that the Church can best protect this revelation through an authoritarian form of organisation. To introduce democracy into this situation would be an unthinkable phenomenon. In this regard, it is important to note that the use of the words authoritarianism and democracy in organisations refers to the way power is exercised and authority established. In an authoritarian system of government, authority is situated in the person who gives the orders. In democratic systems, on the other hand, authority emerges from the mutual exchange between people. In contemporary political and religious bodies, the only place in which authority should be situated is with the whole people.

If these two factors (the rhetoric of institution and authoritarian patterns of power) can be creatively addressed, Moran sees the parish as holding the possibility of being an authentic religious community. This body of people would educate by this *design* of life.

Any discussion on the role of the parish or congregation as an educational community must necessarily recognise that the word *parish* oftentimes refers to different forms of organisation. *Parish*, for example, may be understood as involving several thousands of people and, as a result may require a complex form of organisation. On the other hand, it may comprise a small number of people and, therefore, require very little organisation. In between these two extremes can be found a parish of intermediate size. Gabriel Moran names these parishes as the *super* parish, the *mini* parish and the *intermediate* parish.[12] The super parish is large enough to be organised efficiently and the small parish is small enough to invite everyone's participation. The problem, however, seems to lie with the intermediate parish. Being neither large nor small, it can frequently experience organisational problems in terms of not being able to invite the full participation of each member. Nonetheless, it can benefit from the learnings experienced by both the super and the mini parishes. Whatever the size of the parish, each parish educates if it is designed and organised as a community of small communities.

Moran's work on the parish as educator finds resonance in the writing of John Westerhoff III when he emphasises that the locus of parish religious education is found in the faith community. The content of religious education needs to move from an emphasis on schooling to a community of faith, an example of which is the parish. When this occurs, it is necessary to focus attention on the radical nature of the Church as a faith community.

Believing that 'in a significant community the people share a common memory of tradition, common understandings and ways of life, and common goals and purposes', Westerhoff points to a fourfold argument as to why this is so.[13] First, the existence of such a community requires unity in essentials, as well as a clear identity. It is only within a self-conscious intentional community of faith that a religious way of life can be nurtured.

Secondly, a faith community should be of a size that facilitates meaningful and purposeful interactions among its members. If a particular parish comprises a very large number of families, it is vital to encourage the development of small communities within the large unit. Westerhoff points out that without a sense of intimate community, the local church becomes just another institution within society.

Third, authentic (Christian) community involves the presence and interaction of three generations. The second generation is the generation of the present, the first is that of vision and the third carries the memory. Westerhoff claims that without the presence of the latter, the other two generations are locked into the existential present. 'Without interaction between and among the generations, each making its own unique contribution, Christian community is difficult to maintain.'[14]

Finally, a true Christian community appreciates and encourages the various charisms and gifts among all of its members, just as happened in the early Church. Westerhoff goes so far as to say that 'if one sex is restricted to particular roles or denied equal status, there can be no Christian community.'[15] One must surely question this position, since the implication is that real Christian community cannot exist in the Catholic tradition, since women are excluded from ordination. Gabriel Moran's vision, however, is substantially in accord with Westerhoff's sentiments. In a word, a genuine faith community is the chief educator.

Education through modelling

The second way in which the parish engages in religious education is through modelling. The parish models a way of life. It demonstrates a way of being in the world. This is educative. In educating people to be religious, the Christian parish is concerned with Christian tradition and how this tradition can be handed on. As a religious educator, the parish is involved with handing on a particular tradition and a particular religion. Any attempt to do this must acknowledge the existence of other traditions and religions and the relationship of Christianity to those religions. In order to be effective, Moran believes that 'handing on involves design, reshaping, criticism, and personal response within the process of tradition.'[16] In this regard, it must be noted that what one hands on is not the tradition, but the religion that creates the tradition anew. This is the process of handing on.

People are introduced to a religious way of life from their first moments on earth. Children learn through external routine practice, as well as through absorbing some of the attitudes of adults. Children also learn from the universe and their surrounding environment. They learn from stories and from the way in which they encounter adults. What they need most is that a way of life be made available to them. Their ability to choose how they should respond also needs to be developed. What young people need is an adult community that continues to learn, a community that evinces care and compassion and one that celebrates life-giving liturgies. This is what it means to model a way of life.

From the beginning of Christianity, it was the life and *actions* of Christians in the world that attracted and converted people to the Christian faith. Westerhoff points out that 'we are more apt to learn the implications of faith through the ways we are encouraged and stimulated to act in the world than through our study of Christian ethics.'[17] The vocation of the Christian is lived out in the world as he or she joins God in God's liberating historic actions. The Christian is called to embody Yahweh's work on behalf of justice, love and peace. Therefore, the Church needs to explore the nature and character of members' individual and corporate actions in the world as aspects of its life and to include these actions as part of educational ministry. This educational enterprise should prepare and stimulate members to engage in Christian action. In Westerhoff's words, 'the church is called by God, not to be a community of cultural continuity in support of the status quo but a countercultural community of social change.'[18] In Moran's terms, this is the church educating by modelling a way of life to its members and to the world.

2. The Parish as Teacher

The second theme to be explored in this chapter is the role of the parish as teacher. At the outset, it is important to restate that every human being, as well as some nonhumans, engages in the act of teaching. As Moran puts it, 'teaching is one of the most important and regular acts that we perform in life.'[19] The human person learns through teaching. The most comprehensive meaning of the verb *to teach* is that it shows someone how to live. This understanding also has a religious meaning in that showing people how to live eventually includes showing them how to die.

Teaching, as we have seen, is far broader than furnishing children with explanations. It also includes the teaching done by communities in non-verbal ways, as well as the teaching executed by the nonhuman universe. Contained therein are languages of teaching other than the academic, ones that acknowledge that the majority of the world's teaching is done in a nonverbal and unintentional way. Indeed, every religious tradition is aware of the fact that the young learn about that tradition through their immersion in ritualistic formulas.

The languages of teaching

In discussing the role of the parish as teacher, it is important to recognise that most teaching is nonverbal. By this is meant that words are not the object of the teaching. Teaching, rather, is more concerned with activities, with speech taking on a subordinate role. The development of a religious life, therefore, is taught in the form of silent witness. This is not to say that there is no place for speech in teaching someone to be religious. Speech is always present in community life where the three families of teaching languages are found – homiletic, therapeutic and academic. The presence of these languages, however, is not to dismiss the nonverbal language that exists in any communication between persons. 'Any attempt at religious education', Moran writes, 'that neglects nonverbal symbols would miss the centre of the matter'.[20]

In order to discuss the manner in which the parish engages in teaching people to be religious, it is necessary to revisit these three families of teaching languages. While all three can be found in the parish setting, the languages of the first two families are particularly indispensable. Complex uses of speech are used in all developed religions, with particular mixes of the homiletic and therapeutic emerging in the speech of religious communities. The Christian message is taught through the use of both languages. Joining with the nonverbal forms of teaching, these languages show a person the meaning of living according to this way. To these we now turn.

The parish engages in the therapeutic family of languages by helping to remove any obstacles that may prevent people from hearing the word of God. This may lead people to question what obstacles need removing in parish life and whether they can be removed by teaching. Indeed, the very attempt to remove obstacles may seem unconnected with what it means to teach. Nevertheless, this section will illustrate how, in the parish setting, the therapeutic family of languages is indispensable in showing people how to live and how to die. That is, in the words of Moran, they are salvific. They bring 'the health, wholeness and holiness that religions promise.'[21]

As was previously noted, the therapeutic family of languages engages in calming, soothing and healing. They deal with the essence of human life and, therefore, are central to teaching in a parish setting. These languages require ritual and are particularly pertinent to life's great moments, such as birth, marriage and death. They also calm, soothe and heal in the daily rituals of everyday life.

The therapeutic family of languages does not presuppose that all is well in the parish community. On the contrary, it is aware of the de facto segregation in existence in parish life, together with the individual's quest for truth within this setting. In the course of everyday life, people require the assistance of a language that restores, a language that heals and comforts. The very act of speaking enables the therapeutic process to begin. It invites the speaker to encounter the profound silence located at the centre of speech. This is the essence of therapeutic speech. The therapeutic calms, soothes and heals more by silence than by speech.

It is interesting to note that the figure of the teacher as healer characterised much of tribal religion in by-gone days. In this regard, the teacher had a healing effect on the community. In the parish setting, the teacher today can have the same healing effect.

The teacher in the parish community engages the therapeutic languages of praise/condemn, welcome/thank, confess/forgive, mourn/comfort. Moran proposes this format of pairing in an effort to illustrate the constant giving and receiving in the therapeutic relationship.[22] By this he means that the teacher and learner continually exchange positions. It is in this process that healing is promoted.

Beginning with the paired languages of *praise/condemn*, it can be noted that praise is the natural response of the human person to being human. It evokes a sense of awe and wonder towards the natural environment of the universe, as well as towards human achievement. The parish engages in the language of praise by promoting the need for ritualised times in which praise can be renewed. For example, the Sabbath provides a time of quiet in which people can get in touch with the centre of life and be nourished by a sense of wonder, awe and praise.

Moran pairs *praise* with *to condemn* and views their relationship as one of opposites. The parish, in engaging in the teaching activity, condemns what threatens to destroy the beauty of the universe or interferes with human accomplishment. The unjust structures that breed poverty and suffering deserve to be condemned. However, this action is only the initial step in restoring beauty to the situation. The language of condemnation must also be accompanied by vehement action in order to rectify the state of affairs.

The therapeutic languages of *welcome/thank* are more reciprocal in nature than that of praise/condemn. Beginning from a different assumption, welcome/thank is characterised by an openness to the universe and to all the surprises contained therein. This involves an openness to other human beings, manifested primarily in interpersonal exchanges. The parish engages the language of welcome by promoting welcome as a basic attitude to life and extending it to all people. In the parish setting, no one is a stranger.

Experiences of welcome evoke expressions of gratitude and, thus, thanking is the resultant action of being in the universe. In engaging in the activity of prayer, the parish teaches the meaning of thanksgiving. It is through the rituals of welcome and thanks that the human world can embrace a new day.

The languages of *confess/forgive* are vital when the flow of human life experiences interruption. To this degree, the human person requires the ritual of confession in order to alleviate any stress. The Catholic Church, in providing the sacrament of penance, helps to restore balance, both in the life of the individual and in the life of the community. In this regard, it is important to remember that the language of confession is healing only to the extent that forgiveness has been experienced. It is in the act of forgiveness that the world can be renewed and recreated and people can truly experience reconciliation.

The concluding pair of therapeutic languages comprises *mourn/comfort*. These are the languages that pertain, not only to the final life experience of death and dying, but also to the smaller experiences of letting go encountered on one's journey through life. The teaching role of the parish is vital in these situations. Through the provision of a funeral liturgy, as well as counselling, the parish provides a setting in which a person can come to terms with these moments through the experience of ritual. It is the presence of ritual that enables teaching to be effective in these painful moments. Indeed, it is the presence of ritual that brings comfort and strength to the mourner. A gesture, an embrace, a few kind words are all that is needed to begin the healing process which comfort brings.

In engaging the therapeutic family of teaching languages, the parish attempts to clear the clutter and remove some of the obstacles that prevent people from hearing the message of the gospel. In order to proclaim this message, the congregation enlists the help of another family of languages – the homiletic. These are the languages that emerge from the heart of the community and strive to address the essence of what the community believes. Tapping into the memory of the community, these languages take up the text of the peoples' lives and present them in such a way that the past is linked with the future in the context of the present moment. This is catechesis at its best.

The languages of catechesis comprise storytelling and preaching. Beginning in childhood, storytelling allows the members of the parish community to get in touch with who they are as a people. It reveals to them where they came from and enables them to glimpse where they are going. These are the languages that show a parish how to live and how to die.

Through its engagement in storytelling and preaching, the first family of languages forms an integral part of the liturgical life of the congregation. Ancient rites and formulas are repeatedly recounted, thereby relating the story of the community. Readings from scripture render theory more explicit, while preaching enables the listener to reflect upon these readings. Making use of intimate language, the preacher arouses the hearts of the people and directs them towards acts of justice and compassion. The homilist, therefore, invites the community to put their faith and belief into practice.

Since preaching is an integral part of the parish's liturgical life, Moran provides some guidelines in order to allow preaching to be more effective in the parish setting. First, he encourages preachers to stick to the text. 'The homily is a commentary', he reminds us and, therefore, is preached most effectively when it reflects on the scripture that has just been read.[23] Secondly, the homily must be brief. The preacher can present the essence of the message in a homily that is less than five minutes. To exceed this time may result in boredom for all concerned. A third guideline concerns the manner in which the message is preached. The purpose of the sermon is to challenge the community and, at the same time, inspire them to take action. Therefore, it is important not to nag, scold or complain while delivering a homily. Fourth, Moran advises against using a preachy tone. To do so can detract from the direct, precise and powerful message needing to be heard. Finally, preaching can be more effective when a distinction is made between the roles of priest and preacher. Since the priest is already occupied as presider of the Eucharist and given that not all priests are good preachers, it is recommendable that the talent of other members of the congregation be employed. This is an action that could transform the educative and teaching roles of many parishes.

The third and final family of languages in which the parish engages concerns the academic. Indeed, the three languages involved in teaching the conversation may be used in the parish setting. For example, the language of dramatic performance is pertinent when a gospel story is performed as a play within a play and reflects back on language itself. Secondly, it is not uncommon to find a reading/study group set up in the congregation. When this occurs, dialectical discussion takes place through oral exchange and by reading in such a way that respects the otherness of the text. This is a language that enables parish members to step into the shoes of another human being and experience the world from that point of view.

The language of academic criticism has the potential to be the most powerful of the teaching languages both inside and outside the parish. This is the language of the classroom and takes place within the classroom of the parish. In this setting, academic dialogue takes place between students and teacher. The words of the student become the main focus of reference and the role of the teacher is to design and redesign these words in order to distinguish meaning and promote greater reflection and understanding. This is the setting in which people are taught to understand religion. While this type of teaching is perfectly legitimate in a parish setting, the frequency with which it occurs is minimised by lack of resources and lack of commitment.

In using the language of academic criticism, Moran stresses the importance of distinguishing between the teaching that occurs from the pulpit and the teaching that takes place in the classroom. The homilist invites listeners to put their beliefs into practice; the schoolteacher, on the other hand, cannot tell people what to think or how to behave. Their task, rather, is to explore the meaning of a text and enable students to articulate their own opinions/convictions. Moran verbalises it thus: 'The child who walks into the classroom of a church-related school has a right to expect not catechising but 'rigorous, intellectually demanding accounts of religion.'[24]

In teaching the conversation, the schoolteacher's first step is to present what the Church teaches on a given issue. The second step, however, is to invite dialogue by asking questions concerning the meaning of the teaching and assessing its strengths and weaknesses. This is the essence of classroom teaching and pertains to the activity of any classroom irrespective of whether the school is religiously affiliated or not.

By way of summary, it can be said that schooling in religion for the congregation (young, old and middle-aged) is necessary in order to address the academic side of parish life. The full range of the academic discipline of teaching religion emerges in the adult years. The parish can attend to this need by providing teaching/learning settings in which this can take place. This is an indispensable form of religious education in parish life.

3. The Parish as Moral Educator

The third theme in the role of the parish as religious educator is the manner in which the parish educates morally. The parish educates morally by being a parish. Whatever forms good education in this setting is morally educative. Conversely, whatever is morally educative deserves to be called education. We can say then that the parish or congregation educates morally in two main ways: by design and by example.

Morally educating by design

The design best suited to educating morally in the parish is that of community. The community educates morally by being a democratic community, by being a place where mutuality of power is experienced. The role of community is essential in the moral development of a person. Beginning with the young child, he or she is immersed in the discipline and ways of a community. Children are educated morally by what they see, hear, touch and taste. As a result, they imbibe a sense of right and wrong, a factor on which the future of moral growth is based.

The inter-generational nature of the parish or congregational community enables people to embrace each stage of moral development. It does this by helping them respond to what life offers at every given moment. In this regard, it witnesses to the fact that moral education begins from the first moments of life and continues until death. Now it can be seen that morality and education are essentially the same process.

The formative influence of the parish community is depicted through the creation of a common culture, a culture with shared rituals, symbols and practices. In this regard, Gabriel Moran writes that the moral teachings are about small rituals and ordinary practices that do not seem to have moral content:

> how one dresses and wears one's hair, what one eats and drinks, when one is silent and to whom one speaks, when the time is for sleep and when the time is to awake. These are the disciplines that create communities of moral people.[25]

Seen in this light, the commandments of the Christian Churches may be regarded as statements of address rather than abstract principles. They provide the perimeters within which life is lived.

Moral education within the parish community takes place through a common culture in which rituals, symbols and practices are shared. Some of the ways in which these can be manifested are through Eucharist (the sharing of a common meal), the celebration of large feasts such as Christmas and Easter and during times of recreation such as garden fêtes, picnics fairs. The Eucharist, for example, invites the participation of all parish members. Gathering around the altar provides the opportunity for all to be nourished. It is a place where people learn the meaning of human life and what it means to be in relation to a Creator and to a created life. The common culture of parish life, therefore, is essential to moral education and to the formation of character.

Educating morally by example

The second way in which the parish or congregation educates morally is by example, by modelling a way of life. In its total environment of space, arrangements and interrelations, the parish demonstrates a moral way of being in the world. This is a setting in which nobody is excluded because of gender, race or age. It is a community in which the words of St Paul to the Galatians are taken to heart:

> ... there are no more distinctions between Jew and Greek, slave and free, male and female, but all of you are in Christ Jesus. (3:28).

The total parish population, that is, all who comprise the parish community, teach morally on a daily basis. Most of the time this occurs in an unconscious manner. In this regard, a good test of what the parish teaches by example is to watch the manner in which its members interact.

The parish or congregation educates morally through the way in which it engages in service, in the corporal works of mercy, in acts of peace and justice. These indispensable activities of moral education in parish life overflow from life-giving liturgy. Moran explains that the relation between liturgy and compassionate acts is more 'a rhythm of movement inward toward the quiet centre of a community and movement outward to the dispossessed and suffering' than an association of cause and effect.[26] The Catholic liturgy is designed in such a way as to perpetuate the two traditions of Sabbath found in Hebrew Scriptures. One tradition emphasises the Sabbath as a day of rest, the other demands action for peace and justice. The marriage of these two traditions takes place in the rite of communion experienced at every Eucharist. It serves as a reminder that every creature, both human and nonhuman, is invited to communion, to intimate fellowship. The parish, therefore, models a way of life through its service to the poor and needy. It does this by not counting the cost and by not segregating those who are considered strangers. The role of the parish in these acts of service is to love and care for those in need. It is to prick the conscience of the public at large, as well as to influence government agencies. In engaging in such activities, the parish educates its members in how to live a moral life. The main recipients of education, therefore, are those who give the assistance rather than those who are the receivers.

The ecclesiastical term for service and acts of mercy is *diakonia*. In the New Testament this work refers to service or ministry and is used in two ways. Sometimes it is used in a general sense, referring to the entire range of outreach to others. On other occasions, it carries particular and specific meaning, designating activities such as serving at table, providing hospitality to guests (Matthew 8:15, Luke 4:39 and 8:3), or acting on behalf of the poor, (Romans 15:31).

Maria Harris complements Moran's description of service by focusing on the second meaning of diakonia – providing a particular and specific service and outreach to others. In doing this, however, she does not lose sight of its more general connotation. Her intention is 'toward remembering and integrating compassionate service as part of the essential curricular work of every Christian community, while recalling at the same time the interconnectedness of all works of ministry within the pastoral vocation.'[27] She emphasises that the obligation of service and outreach is the work of the entire community and not just those who have designated offices in the parish. It is a work of compassionate ministry, both directly to persons and structurally toward unjust systems, a factor critical to any community of faith.

Harris warns against fostering guilt as part of the curriculum of diakonia. Instead, graceful and compassionate giving should stem from an attitude of gratitude for life and freedom and a joyful appreciation of all that one has been given, together with the recognition that abundance is not shared equally. The power of compassion is at the root of the fashioning of a curriculum of service. This compassionate stance was profoundly modelled by Jesus of Nazareth. Jesus, named the Christ, saw that washing feet, healing the sick and feeding the hungry were natural and necessary.

Harris names four forms of diakonia, whose presence in the curriculum educates *to* ministries of service and *by* ministries of service. They comprise social care, social ritual, social empowerment and social legislation.

Social care: Like Moran, Harris believes that the exercise of care involves, not only the one who is caring, but also the one receiving the care. Caring is a way of being and doing which necessarily involves both parties. In this regard, she writes 'care makes us receivers as well as givers: the one who is caring is always a part of, and within, the caring activity. Thus, it is essentially social.'[28] Care is rooted in three attitudes that are central to the curriculum of community and the curriculum of prayer: relation, receptivity and response. These are attitudes that make a positive contribution to the social order and the social fabric.

Social ritual: According to Harris, 'social rituals are organised actions characterised by regular, patterned, artistic movement involving groups of people bonded together in reaching out.'[29] In other words, people fashion diakonia when, as groups and communities, they come together in organised ways, such as vigils, marches, parades and prayer services, to protest situations that minimise the care demanded by the Gospel.

Social empowerment: A third and essential form of diakonia involves working toward structural change, that is changing the social systems and social policies that perpetuate injustice. In this way victims of injustice are enabled to claim their own power. Harris states that 'the important point concerning social empowerment is that its emphasis is not on what the caregivers do, but on conditions where the needy are able to take responsibility for themselves.'[30]

Social legislation: It should be clear at this stage that actions of social care, ritual and empowerment must be twofold. First, they must address the actual situations of injustice at home and abroad by providing practical help. Secondly, diakonia must correspondingly address the structural causes that perpetuate unjust conditions. It follows that structures for permanent diakonia that has end (meaning) and yet is always without end (termination) are necessary since marginalisation is a permanent feature of our world. 'Thus', as Harris states, 'although diakonia is prophetic in its attention to care, priestly in its impulse toward ritual, and both of these in its attention to empowerment, each of these forms is incomplete unless it is also political.'[31] Only when existing institutions that prevent people from living complete human lives are refashioned will permanent positive social change occur. One effective way to do this is through political action. Through the curriculum of diakonia, Church leaders and Church communities are called to become involved in civic life and continually monitor social legislation in order to ensure that it promotes true justice and truly educates in a moral fashion. Harris here has simply extended Moran's thesis: the parish/congregation educates morally by example, especially by the example of service.

The parish, as we have seen, educates morally by design and by modelling. Let us turn now to three specific ways in which this occurs within the parish or congregational setting – teaching morally, teaching morality and teaching morality (ethics) in the classroom of the church.

Teaching morally

As I have mentioned, people are continually questioning whether it is possible to teach morally. This is due to the widespread suspicion that teaching is an immoral act. Such a premise has arisen from the typical image of teaching punctuating educational theory – that of an adult schoolteacher, usually a woman, telling a child what to do and think. Gabriel Moran addresses the problem of teaching morally by distancing himself from classroom teaching and examining the meaning of teaching as it occurs in ordinary everyday life. The basic meaning of 'to teach' is, as we have seen, to show someone how to do something. This is an activity that, at first glance, connotes no moral conflict. The reason for this is that the universe, in offering daily gifts, is the most comprehensive teacher. It is only when the teacher moves from the universe to the human community that the potential for moral conflict arises. The cause of this potential conflict is due to the incomplete and imperfect nature of the human community. To this end, the parish community is no exception.

The full emergence of the moral problem with regard to teaching emerges when a person is presented as 'the teacher'. This is not to imply that teaching is an immoral act. Rather, it points to the fact that when the teacher is aware of the conditions under which he or she can legitimately teach, then teaching is a morally good activity. As Moran puts it, 'if one is attentive to the several forms of teaching and the language appropriate to each form, it is possible to teach morally.'[32] By this he means that there is a time and place for each of the teaching modes. For example, within the parish or congregational context, it is appropriate to use the homiletic family of languages in the liturgical setting. This is the language best suited to the ministry of the word and to catechesis. To allow these languages to dominate in another setting, such as in a counselling situation or in the classroom, would be inappropriate, that is, immoral. Similarly, to use the languages of therapy or academic criticism in the liturgical setting would also constitute the overstepping of boundaries. Teaching, therefore, becomes immoral when boundaries are overstepped. In a word, teaching morally means showing how to do the right thing in the right setting.

Teaching morality

How, therefore, does the parish teach morality? In order to answer this question, Moran examines the manner in which the teaching of morality occurs throughout the great religions of the world. First, however, it is interesting to note the diversity in rituals and practices that exists across the major world religions. Despite this diversity, however, remarkable similarity exists in the manner in which these religions educate morally. To this end, Moran isolates some characteristics that are woven through some of these great systems.

First, throughout the major world religions, it is the leader, the master, the guru who is given the title *teacher*. This is a person, whose life is an inspiration and an embodiment of authority, who becomes the source of moral education. They lure the hearts of people, not so much by what they say, but by their presence. In the Jewish tradition, it was Moses who was the great teacher. In Christianity, it was Jesus of Nazareth.

Secondly, these great teachers do not focus on the great problems of the world. Rather, they concentrate on the daily lives of a small group of people. The teacher, in sharing a way of life with these people, provides moral guidance. The result is that moral education occurs osmotically through the ritual of daily living. The homiletic languages of teaching are prominent in this setting, but are only secondary to the teaching done by example.

A third characteristic concerns living within a discipline. The great religions of the world teach morality through engagement in rituals that, on the surface, appear to be totally divorced from morality. However, what these great teachers know is that the discipline of daily rituals teach disciples the fabric of what it means to be in relationship with others. It is within the community setting that they learn the meaning of care, respect, gratitude, compassion.

Fourth, religions seek to promote unity between the self and the cosmos. By this is meant that, while rules may appear to dominate in a religious way of life, religions regard morality as moving beyond rules of behavior to the rights of all living things in the universe. Everything that breathes stands in relation to everything that constitutes the universe. All deserve care and respect from the human community. In this regard, Moran writes

> the moral life is mainly one of 'discriminating', that is, of perceiving differences between human beings who call forth a wide range of response depending on whether the person is parent, spouse, child, friend, stranger. Every human and nonhuman being equally deserves that we should care, but only the precise context can specify how.[33]

In other words, the vocation of the human community is to discern its relation to the nonhuman world and come to the realisation that we form a unity. Failure to do this results in human beings who do not realise their potential for wholeness.

Finally, the great religions of the world perceive moral education as lifelong. For them, moral education begins at birth and continues until the moment of death. From infancy, people's lives are shaped by their physical and social environment and moral education takes place through the care they receive and experience as they grow towards maturity.

Teaching morality within the parish or congregation ought to emulate the example depicted by the great world religions. They reveal the fact that the moral life is taught by the parish that has character and virtue. In other words, the parish teaches morality by being a virtuous community and a community of character. According to Moran, virtue and care will lead people back to character and community. Virtue, meaning strength, is procured through repetition and understanding, through engaging in the rituals of daily life. The virtuous congregation or parish, therefore, is one that has integrated its strengths.

The parish develops character by responding to the social environment and to the needs of others. In developing virtue and character, the parish provides a parish/community narrative, thereby laying the foundation for moral development. In so doing, the parish provides a story and makes it feasible for parishioners to know and own their particular story. In this way, members are helped to value their common beliefs, as well as to accept the principles of behavior, manners of address and modes of being together. These are manifested particularly in the sharing of celebrations, as well as in times of sorrow.

As moral educator, the parish leads its members to respond to the present moment in a way that is faithful and careful. The parish now becomes a place where understanding and imagination are both deepened and expanded. The ethic of virtue and care, character and community, is taught primarily through inspiration and imitation. Parish members absorb the attitudes and behaviours expected of them. They become moral people by sharing in the life of a moral parish. Now we can see that it is not just church officials who educate morally. Rather, each parishioner educates each parishioner towards moral character. In this regard, any given parishioner may assume the role of teacher on any given issue at any given time.

In summary, therefore, we can say that morality is taught when the parish/congregation is responsible, relational and in accordance with nature. The parish acts responsibly by being responsible to the available truth. It teaches that responsible morality is relational in that it is aware of the many relations that touch its life. And it teaches morality when it is in accordance with nature, that is when the natural is not rejected or destroyed.

Teaching morality (ethics) in the classroom of the Church
The academic form of teaching morality takes place in the classroom and falls under what is commonly named 'ethics'. In

this environment the language employed involves teaching the conversation. While one learns conversation simply by belonging to the human community, teaching the conversation is a specific language in which the language of teaching is examined. This occurs through questioning the meaning of beliefs in an effort to unlock what lies below the surface. In order to elucidate what he means by this, Moran, as we saw, includes three languages in this family of teaching languages. They comprise dramatic performance, dialectical discussion and academic criticism. The language of dramatic performance is used when a play is found within a play or when a play reflects on storytelling or other forms of speech. In this situation, teaching becomes a reflection on language itself. Dialectical discussion attempts to reflect on dialectical moments, inviting a person to walk in the shoes of another and experience the world from that point of view. Finally, the third language in this family of languages concerns academic criticism. Comprising all the languages of teaching, this language focuses on the words of the student, allowing them to become the main point of reference and the focus of criticism.

Teaching the conversation in the classroom of the parish or congregation, therefore, attends to the language of the classroom. Involving critical conversation, this teaching language invites the questioning of meaning and is born out of profound reflection. This is a language that avoids the languages of preaching and the therapeutic. Rather, it becomes a process of schooling in which sustained discussion is the focus of teaching and people are enabled to attain a discernment of their own.

In attempting to teach the conversation, the parish or congregation may well ponder over what to teach. Moran throws some light on this dilemma when he explores the issue of what the religions teach about morality. In acknowledging the fundamental differences religions have in this area, he offers what he considers to be the ultimate foundation of morality from a religious point of view: 'what is unnatural is immoral'.[34]

This statement, Moran believes, finds a home in most, if not all, the world religions. All moral issues can be viewed and assessed through this perspective.

However, the question arises of what it means to act unnaturally. For example, in the past people did not appreciate the fact that polluting a river was an unnatural act. Today, that is considered to be an unnatural act. Conversely, people heretofore considered homosexuality to be contrary to nature. Today, it is regarded as a variation in the human condition.

Based on a care for nature, religious morality is concerned about the uniqueness of each organism and the place it occupies in the fabric of life. The human vocation rests on this belief and finds a home in the Christian and Jewish religions that recognise a superiority to human life. In this view, the human person is the only morally responsible creature. Acknowledgment of this fact, however, is not to place the human being on top or to give him or her an authoritarian role over the rest of creation. Rather, it is based on the essence of teaching in the Book of Genesis when man and woman are placed at the centre of all living organisms, responsible for the gentle transformation of the world.

The parish, with its own particular relations, provides the people with a moral community from which they can respond to the organic relations of the biotic system. It provides the springboard from which people become aware of each organism's right to existence and their own ontological vocation not to destroy. Paradoxically, the human vocation includes killing in the sense of breathing, walking on the earth's surface, eating what once lived.

In summary, therefore, it can be said that teaching morality (ethics) in the classroom of the parish or congregation provides a venue in which to discuss the great moral issues of our time. People require a setting in which they can discuss issues that impact on their lives, issues such as bioethics, ecology, sexism. The categories of natural and unnatural can be a moral lens to critically assess these aspects of life. This is not the place where people are told the truth. The role of the teacher, rather, is to facilitate discussion. It is to shed light on these pertinent issues by sharing the insights of the Church, as well as inviting the voices of the people, both inside and outside the parish. In other words, the teacher in this setting facilitates the discussion in such a way as to enable people to reach a discernment of their own. Success is measured by a better understanding of the topic discussed and the congregation's arriving at their own decisions.

The Parish as Educator and Teacher

In educating adults, it is important to question the ideal of adulthood towards which one is being educated. The manner in which many institutions and educational theories put adults and children in opposition reveals a narrow assumption of adulthood. In becoming adult, it is assumed that one leaves behind the spontaneous and playful characteristics of childhood and adopts the rational, independent and productive qualities of adulthood. While these qualities are not to be bemoaned, they fail to furnish a complete and realistic picture of adulthood. Indeed, this attitude was not helped by the introduction of the term *adult education*, a term that is frequently misleading in that it seems to connote only two age groups – children and adults. To complicate matters, in the past, the task of adult education was assigned to the Churches in the hope of curbing the thinking and actions of adults. The result was that education within the parish tended to be child-centred, leading, in turn, to the Church becoming a childish Church.

The reality of a childish Church is not to be confused with the positive meaning of what it means to be childlike, a meaning that does not stand in opposition to the rational, independent and productive. Throughout religious history, for example, the attitude of childlike has had special significance. 'Unless you become like a little child', Jesus said, 'you cannot enter the Kingdom of God.' This is a statement that brought the childlike to the centre of the Christian gospel. Interestingly, this statement did not pertain to children but to adults. It is not to be confused with the exhortation by Paul in 1 Corinthians 13:11 to put all childish things away.

Segregating people into either adults or children, therefore, is not a helpful distinction. In response to this dilemma, Gabriel Moran believes that it is necessary to have an education that brings about their unity. 'Forms which unite the ages', he writes, 'ought to be the primary focus for thinking about education, especially in churches.'[35] This leads him to call for finer distinctions, distinctions that 'recognise the existence of infants, children, youth, young adults, middle adults and older children.'[36] The congregation, having access to all ages of the population, might respond to this challenge by demonstrating a different form of education. Learning within an intergenerational context enables the ideal of adulthood to be understood by peoples of all ages. It is a learning in which people can work towards 'an integration of dependence and independence, the rational and the nonrational, life and death.'[37] When this occurs, all formation is directed towards the ideal of adulthood characterised by Christian maturity. The result would be an adulthood-centred church.

Loretta Girzaitis strongly supports Moran's ideal of adulthood. Exploring the meaning of the word *adult*, she writes that it comes from the Latin word *adolescere*, meaning *to grow up*.[38] Such an understanding of adulthood implies action, continuous growth towards wholeness and integrity. Growth towards adulthood is an invitation extended to every human person. It is a journey travelled in the company of the whole human race.

The journey towards adulthood is marked by certain characteristics. Chief among these are the ability of adults to learn new behaviour, to cope with the various crises they encounter, to reflect upon life and determine the necessary changes, and to interplay the external and internal events of life – all of which reveal that maturation is a lifelong process. Questioning what dimension the churches add to the process of adult maturity, Girzaites points out that while members share the state of humanity with every human being, they have the added dimension of Jesus' companionship, as well as the experience of community in worship, mission and service.

Evelyn E. Whitehead and James D. Whitehead also emphasise that people grow *towards* adulthood rather than *in* adulthood.[39] Their belief is that the achievement of psychological and religious maturity is dependent on one's creative response to loss and failure and results in the ability to be loving and generative. This, according to them, is the essence of religious maturity, the ideal of adulthood towards which the Churches educate.

Adult Growth and Church Authority

Current patterns of authority in the Church may pose problems for any parish or congregation who direct their educational efforts toward Christian maturity. The more people are educated towards adulthood, the more threatening it is for Church authorities. James R. Schaefer, for example, directly engages the conflict between contemporary principles of adult learning and growth and the tradition of authority exercised by the Catholic Church.[40] In this regard, he bluntly questions whether the Church can endure the emergence of mature believers and emphasises that adult religious *education*, as opposed to *indoctrination*, would introduce unbearable tensions and strains within the Church. 'The tension', he writes, 'is between Roman Catholic traditions of authority on the one hand and, on the other, adult education principles which emphasise self-direction.'[41] The conflict, therefore, concerns ideological, rather than hierarchical, differences, and concerns the degree to which people can be autonomous in their beliefs and decisions within the Roman Catholic community.

There are two levels at which this problem surfaces – the theological/philosophical level and the practical level. Thus, the dilemma lies with both orthodoxy and orthopraxis. The theological/philosophical level concerns at least three issues: development of doctrine, personhood and adult learning principles, with the problem lying between doctrine and human tradition. The practical level, on the other hand, situates the conflict between the Church's authoritative moral teaching and peoples' varying ethical convictions. Schaefer puts the matter thus:

> The most obvious manifestation of the problem at the practical level is the conflict between authoritative moral teaching on the one hand, and variant decisions of conscience on the other. It is not just a matter of people deciding to do something that authoritative teaching says is wrong. It is a matter of people believing the action is right.[42]

The religiously mature adult, therefore, makes a conscientious decision to balance Church teaching and the realistic facts of the given situation.

James Bacik takes this matter further by raising the fundamental question of whether the terms *Christian* and *maturity* are compatible or whether they are, in fact, antithetical.[43] Indeed, many influential writers of the nineteenth and twentieth centuries, including Karl Marx, Friedrich Nietzche, Sigmund Freud and Jean-Paul Sartre, have contended that the terms are essentially contradictory. These four masters of suspicion portrayed Christianity as being essentially dehumanising and, therefore, detrimental to one's growth towards maturity. Their influence, together with the negative effects of patriarchal society present a challenge in the effort to attain Christian maturity. What is needed is 'a credible ideal of maturity that can overcome all the changes that religion is essentially dehumanising and that Christianity is inevitably sexist.'[44]

Christianity, on the other hand, illustrates how *Christianity* and *maturity*, rather than being antithetical, are in fact mutually exclusive. This can be seen through: 1) the person of Jesus who models the essence of what it means to be a mature person; 2) Scriptures' reminder that one's ontological calling is to strive towards maturity in the service of others; and 3) the Documents of Vatican II where the call to Christian maturity is based upon our dignity as human beings. With such an understanding of maturity one does not experience a reduction of freedom but, rather, a liberation to pursue life with greater meaning.

Recognising the lifelong journey required by the maturation process, Christian humanists, and Karl Rahner in particular, understand the mature individual as integrating opposites and holding them in fruitful tension. Rahner's anthropology suggests that the journey towards Christian maturity necessitates the development of such dialectical virtues as committed openness, reflective spontaneity, hopeful realism, enlightened simplicity and prayerfully prophetic. Positioned between tendencies characterising immaturity, these dialectical virtues illustrate how opposing tendencies can be dialectical in character and produce a synthesis that is both life-giving and energising.

In redesigning its pattern of power and authority and creating a more communal form of life, the Church could embrace the ideal of adulthood towards which all are invited. In working together towards this ideal, church authorities no longer feel threatened and the maturing faithful experience support in pursuing their quest. In this scenario, the whole Christian community will educate the whole Christian community toward greater human integration and wholeness. This is what St. Paul means by 'to grow up in Christ.'

The Parish as Educator, Teacher and Moral Educator

The parish as educator, teacher and moral educator educates towards adulthood by being aware of, facilitating and supporting three religious educational stages and six emerging moments that occur in the life of a human person on the journey from birth to death. Moran outlines these stages as follows.[45] Entitled *simply religious*, the primordial stage of religious education at begins from the first moments of life and continues for approximately five to seven years. This stage comprises two main moments – the physical and the mythical – and takes place primarily in family life. The physical moment permeates the whole organism and is experienced in the ways love, affection and, indeed, all physical contact is manifested to the infant both before and after birth. In this way, it sows the seeds of openness to receive whatever life may bring. From the religious perspective, the child experiences life as never-ending mystery, with the divine suffusing the daily miracles of life. At this stage, the child learns two important characteristics, each of which shapes one's attitude towards life – that all is gift and that salvation does not occur in isolation, but in the context of community. The family's role is to protect and nurture the infant/child in his or her indigenous religiousness.

The second moment of this first stage of religious education development concerns the mythical. Complementing the physical moment, the mythical manifests itself in the form of imagery and stories. Not having any concept of a personal God, the child, at this stage, perceives God or even gods as being present in the universe. For them, all intense experiences are manifestations of the power of the divine. Religious experience, therefore, can be a source of happiness, but it can also be filled with terror. This fear, however, can be alleviated when presented in the form of story and image. Fairy tales are an invaluable resource here and assure the child of the triumph of good over evil. The family can contribute here by good story-telling and even introducing some elementary form of biblical stories.

The second stage of religious education development towards adulthood concerns the acquisition of religion and comprises the two moments of *our people's belief* and *disbelief.* During this time children begin to separate what, to them, had previously been united. For example, they can now differentiate between what is living and what is not, between what is human and what is not. It is during this stage that the child's capacity to collect and accumulate information is developed, as well as his or her ability to think abstractly. The school setting, therefore, is key during this stage of education towards adulthood.

In moving from the primordial stage of religiousness, the child grapples with some of the mysteries of the universe and begins to ask questions in an effort to know *our people's belief.* The answers to these questions come from parents, teachers and the parish community and give the child a sense of belonging to a people with a past. The narrative now becomes historical in character and enables the child to identify with a particular people. The Christian story is manifested in this way and, in this regard, the presence of a parish or congregation is invaluable. It is here that the child encounters storytelling in the text of the sacred scriptures. During this stage of acquiring a religion, the young person builds up a system of beliefs, a set of rituals and ethical practices. This is catechesis. As the person proceeds towards religious maturity, the intrusion of reality provokes the adolescent into questioning these beliefs. The result is an examination and a dismantling of the belief system. This is a moment of *disbelief* in which the young person begins to discredit the recently acquired beliefs. At this stage, the beliefs are experienced as too restricting and confining for the journey towards adulthood. This is a stage that should not be perceived as threatening to either young people themselves or to those responsible for them. Rather, the questioning of beliefs is necessary in order that more profoundly religious questions may be postulated. Schooling in religion (or teaching the conversation) is precisely what young people need at this time in their lives. It is in conversing on their questions that leads the young person to the third stage of adult religiousness. The parish needs to provide spaces for this conversation to take place.

The parish also forms the setting for the third stage of religious education towards adulthood. This stage marks the individual's reclaimation of some of the best attitudes of childhood and manifests itself in the manner in which the person is religious is a particular way, that is, particularly Christian, Jewish, Muslim. The two resulting moments in this stage comprise *parable* and *detachment*.

The title *parable* here is indicative of the outlook and mode of speech characterising the early part of this third stage. Setting their hearts on a goal, people reclaim the storytelling of childhood and use parables in order to reflect upon the paradoxes of life. People experience themselves, once again, as belonging to a specific group and being part of a particular history. Noting the difference between parable and storytelling, Moran writes that 'a parabolic attitude is the recognition that the search for answers must go on but with a different expectation of success.'[46] In other words, there is no single answer to a particular problem and life can never be reduced to a rational system. Life must be lived within the tension of the story itself and the religious person must act in the best way he or she can. All absolutes have been shed. There is *not* only one way (of being religious).

Detachment marks the second moment in adult religiousness and is characterised by the willingness to wait. By that is meant that one no longer seeks reward for one's actions. Rather, the religious mature person adheres to one's calling in life and returns any glory received to the Creator. This is not a stage reserved for the saintly few, but is experienced by all those who have come to terms with life and death. Maturity is now characterised by a fusion of all elements of life. In a word, the individual has become religiously mature. The parish's life of prayer and religious ritual moves to the centre here. Zones of quiet, silence, meditation and contemplation are the chief forms of education. These forms of religious education prepare the person to let go of all and die into God.

Conclusion

This chapter has illustrated the crucial role of the parish in the religious education of its members. The parish educates religiously in a unique way – by design and by modelling. It educates by being a religious body (community) and through the manner in which it models a life of prayer and service. People are taught to be religious through employing the teaching languages of the therapeutic, the homiletic and the academic in the parish setting. Ultimately, religious education within the parish is directed to educating people towards religious maturity.

EPILOGUE:
WHAT NEXT?

This book acknowledges that religious education is one of the most important issues facing our world today. It also recognises that the narrow understanding of the meaning and purpose of religious education, together with the babel of languages used to describe what is taking place have contributed to a lack of clarity and a domestication of an activity that pertains to the centre of human life.

Relying heavily on the work of Gabriel Moran, I have sought to bring about linguistic clarity by exploring the meaning of words and challenging the practice of interchanging terms. In calling for an adequate theory of religious education, I chose to work with three major themes running through Moran's educational thought: 1) the meaning and forms of education; 2) the meaning and forms of teaching, and 3) moral education and educating morally. Theme I, *the meaning and forms of education*, aired dissatisfaction with current educational language which narrowly perceives school as *the* form of education and, therefore, pertaining to five to eighteen year olds. In order to broaden this understanding, a lifelong educational form is proposed, one that comprises family, schooling, work and leisure and each of these partially embodies the educational values of community, knowledge, work and wisdom.

Theme II, *the meaning and forms of teaching*, illustrated that teaching embraces more than schoolteaching. In its most comprehensive meaning, the verb 'to teach' entails showing someone how to do something. In this regard, three families of teaching languages were employed – homiletic, therapeutic and academic – all of which show someone how to live and how to die.

The third theme addressed *moral education and educating morally*. Including all the forms of life that educate, an educational morality explores what it means to teach morally, teach morality and teach morality (ethics) in the classroom. These three themes culminate and find expression in an education towards adulthood, that is, one that proposes an ideal of adulthood that incorporates psychological, social and religious maturity.

The book then proceeds into a new paradigm. An educational framework is presented in an attempt to open dialogue within and beyond the Churches. A second language in which to speak about religious education is offered and religious education is understood as comprising two complementary but differing aims: 1) to teach religion and 2) to teach to be religious.

Thus understood, religious education was then examined in three different settings, with the above three educative themes interwoven through each one. The first setting examined the unique role of the family as religious educator. Here, the family's role as educator, teacher and moral educator was explored through the way the family is designed, models a way of life and engages in languages of teaching. Within this environment, people are taught to be religious in a particular way. The predominant teaching languages in this setting are the homiletic and the therapeutic, although the academic can also be present.

The second setting in which religious education was examined concerns the school. Schooling as religious education needs to be open to people of all ages and, therefore, not confined to those aged between five to eighteen years. The unique way in which the school educates is through the language of the academic. This is the language used in teaching people to understand religion. However, while academic criticism particularly pertains to the classroom, the homiletic and therapeutic families of languages may be used in other areas of the school setting.

In discussing the role of the parish in religious education, I explored the unique way in which the parish educates religiously by design and by modelling a way of life. In this regard, the parish as a religious body (community) was discussed and attention given to the manner in which it models a life of prayer and service. The threefold teaching languages of the therapeutic, the homiletic and the academic were proposed as ways of teaching to be religious. Ultimately, the aim of religious education within the parish is to educate people towards religious maturity.

It is the interplay of religious education within family, school and parish that gives rise to a new understanding of and engagement in religious education. At this stage it is appropriate to suggest some educational principles or guidelines that both recognise and honour new directions in religious education.

1   Attention must be paid to consistent educational clarity in the use of the term *religious education*.
2   It is imperative to recognise the two very distinct, but interdependent, aims of religious education: to understand religion and the formation of a person into a religious way of life.
3   While both can be mutually supportive, these two very different processes of religious education – the academic process and the formation process – are two very different processes and, therefore, have very different aims, objectives and purposes.

4 It is essential to recognise that there are different settings for religious education – the school setting is where one is taught to understand religion, while the family and parish settings are where one is taught to be religious.

5 Religious education affirms family, school and parish as religious educators and provides an opportunity to reshape the process of religious education in each setting.

6 The multiple settings for religious education are an invitation to re-imagine the meaning of teaching.

7 Central to religious education is attention to lifestyle, a lifestyle that involves formation towards a virtuous character.

8 All religious education is education towards adulthood, that is towards psychological, social and religious maturity – in other words towards the Kingdom of God.

In summary then, this book has examined the identity of religious education and the corpus of Gabriel Moran's writings has been the vehicle for unveiling the richest possible meaning of religious education for our time.

NOTES

Chapter 1

1   See P.M. Devitt, *That You May Believe*. (Dublin: Dominican Publications, 1992).

2   J.R. Walsh, *Religion: The Irish Experience* (Dublin: Veritas, 2003), p. 25.

3   G. Moran, *Design for Religion* (New York: Herder & Herder, 1971); 'Two Languages of Religious Education'. *The Living Light, 14*, pp. 40-50; *No Ladder to the Sky* (San Francisco: Harper & Row, 1987a); *Religious Education as a Second Language* (Birmingham, Alabama: Religious Education Press, 1989).

4   K. Scott, 'Three Traditions of Religious Education'. *Religious Education, 79*, 1984, pp. 323-339.

5   G. Moran, *Interplay*. (Winona, Minnesota: St. Mary's Press, 1981), p. 21.

6   G. Moran, 'Religious Education' in M. Eliade (Ed.), *Encyclopedia of Religion, Vol. 12*, (New York: Macmillan, 1987b), pp. 318-323.

7   T.H. Groome, *Christian Religious Education*, (San Francisco: Harper & Row, 1980), p. 22.

8   Ibid, p. 25.

9   Ibid, p. 25.

10 B. Marthaler, 'Toward a Revisionist Model of Catechetics', *The Living Light, 13*, 1976, p. 459.

11 T.H. Groome, *Christian Religious Education*, (San Francisco: Harper & Row, 1980), p. 27.

12 Ibid, p. 27.

13 Ibid, p. 27.

14   M.C. Boys, 'Religious Education: A Map of the field' in M.C. Boys, *Education for Citizenship and Discipleship*, (New York: Pilgrim Press, 1989), p. 108.

15   Ibid, p. 124.

16   C. Ellis Nelson, *Where Faith Begins*, (Atlanta, Georgia: John Knox Press, 1971).

17   R. Crump Miller, *The Theory of Christian Education Practice*, (Birmingham, Alabama: Religious Education Press, 1980).

18   M.C. Boys, 'Religious Education: A map of the field' in M.C. Boys (Ed.), *Education for Citizenship and Discipleship*, (New York: Pilgrim Press, 1989), p. 75.

19   K. Scott, 'Communicative competence and religious education', *Lumen Vitae, 35*. 1980, p. 75.

20   Ibid, p. 75.

21   National Conference of Catholic Bishops, *Sharing the Light of Faith*. National Catechetical Directory for Catholics of the United States. (Washington, DC: United States Catholic Conference, 1979), No. 5, p.3.

22   K. Scott, 'Communicative Competence and Religious Education', *Lumen Vitae, 35*, 1980, p. 82.

23   Ibid. p. 83.

24   K. Scott, 'Catechesis and Religious Education: Uncovering the Nature of our Work', *PACE, 12*, 1981a. pp. 1-4.

25   Ibid, p. 1.

26   Ibid, p. 1.

27   Ibid, p. 2.

28   Ibid, p. 2.

29   K. Scott, 'Communicative Competence and Religious Education', *Lumen Vitae, 35*, 1980, p. 83.

30   G. Moran, 'Religious Education' in M. Eliade (Ed.), *Encyclopedia of Religion*, Vol. 12. (New York: Macmillan, 1987a), p. 318.

31   Ibid, p. 319.

32   Ibid, p. 319.

33   Ibid, p. 319.

34   Ibid, p. 319.

35   K. Barker, *Religious Education, Catechesis and Freedom*, (Birmingham, Alabama: Religious Education Press, 1981), p. 27.

36   J. Dewey, *Democracy and Education*, (New York: Free Press, 1966). Original work published in 1908. Quoted in G. Moran, *Interplay*, (Winona, Minnesota: St. Mary's Press, 1981), p. 29.

37 G.A. Coe, *A Social Theory of Religious Education*, (New York: Charles Scribner's Sons, 1917), p. 20.

38 H. Shelton Smith, *Faith and Nurture*, (New York: Charles Scribner's Sons, 1941), p. vii.

39 G. Moran, 'Religious Education' in M. Eliade (Ed.) *Encyclopedia of Religion, Vol. 12, 1987b*, (New York: Macmillan), p. 322.

40 Ibid, p. 41.

41 Ibid, p. 42.

42 Ibid, p. 43.

43 Ibid, p. 43.

44 Ibid, p. 43.

45 Ibid, pp. 40-50.

46 Ibid, p. 46.

47 Ibid, p. 47.

48 G. Moran, *Religious Education as a Second Language*, (Birmingham, Alabama: Religious Education Press, 1989), p. 218.

49 E. Nesbitt, 'Representing faith traditions in religious education: an ethnographic perspective' in *The Fourth R For The Third Millennium*, (Dublin: Lindisfarne Books, 2001), pp. 137-158.

50 G. Moran, *Religious Education as a Second Language*, (Birmingham, Alabama: Religious Education Press, 1989), p. 234.

Chapter 2

1 G. Moran, *Religious Education As A Second Language*, (Birmingham, Alabama: Religious Education Press, 1989), p. 32.

2 G. Moran, *Showing How: The Act of Teaching*, (Valley Forge, PA: Trinity Press International, 1997b).

3 Ibid, p. 152.

4 Ibid, p. 153.

5 B. Bailyn, *Education in the Forming of American Society*, (New York: Vintage Books, 1960).

6 G. Moran, *Showing How: The Art of Teaching*, (Valley Forge, Pa: Trinity Press International, 1997b), p. 39.

7 Ibid, p. 155.

8 F. Newmann & D. Oliver, 'Education and Community' in T. Sizer (Ed.), *Religion and Public Education*. (Boston: Houghton Mifflin, 1967). pp. 184-227.

9 Gabriel Moran, *Showing How: The Act of Teaching*, p. 40.

10 Ibid, p. 35.

11   Ibid, p. 154.

12   G. Moran, *Education Toward Adulthood,* (New York: Paulist Press, 1979). p. 44.

13   Ibid, p. 47.

14   Ibid, p. 52.

15   G. Moran, *Showing How: The Act of Teaching,* (Valley Forge, Pa: Trinity Press International, 1997b), p. 166.

16   G. Moran, *Interplay,* (Winona, Minnesota: St. Mary's Press, 1981). p. 80.

17   Ibid, p. 80.

18   Ibid, pp. 80-81.

19   G. Moran, *Religious Education Development,* (Minneapolis, MN: Winston Press, 1983), p. 166.

20   G. Moran, *Showing How: The Act of Teaching,* (Valley Forge, PA: Trinity Press International, 1997), p. 156.

21   Ibid, pp. 157-158.

22   Ibid, p. 156.

23   Ibid, p. 3.

24   Ibid, p. 5.

25   Ibid, p. 1.

26   Ibid, p. 2.

27   Ibid, p. 3.

28   Ibid, p. 3.

29   Ibid, p. 3.

30   G. Moran, *Religious Body,* (New York: The Seabury Press, 1974), p. 162.

31   Ibid, p. 163.

32   Ibid, p. 164.

33   Ibid, p. 165.

34   M. Harris & G. Moran, *Reshaping Religious Education,* (Louisville, KY: Westminster/John Knox Press, 1998), p.32

35   Ibid, p. 32.

36   G. Moran, *Showing How: The Act of Teaching,* (Valley Forge, PA: Trinity Press International, 1997), p. 43.

37   Ibid, p. 43.

38   M. Oakeshott, 'Learning and Teaching' in T. Fuller (Ed.), *The Voice of Liberal Learning,* (New Haven: Yale University Press, 1989), pp. 38-49.

39   G. Moran, *Showing How: The Act of Teaching,* (Valley Forge, PA: Trinity Press, International, 1997), p. 44.

40   Ibid, p. 48.

41   Ibid, p. 57.
42   Ibid, p. 70.
43   Ibid, p. 60.
44   Ibid, p. 61.
45   Ibid, p. 79.
46   M. Harris & G. Moran, *Reshaping Religious Education,* (Louisville, KY: Westminster/John Knox Press, 1998), p. 34.
47   G. Moran, *Showing How: The Act of Teaching,* (Valley Forge, PA: Trinity Press International, 1997), p. 87.
48   Ibid, p. 87.
49   Ibid, p. 87.
50   Ibid, p. 95.
51   Ibid, p. 100.
52   Ibid, p. 102.
53   Ibid, p. 111.
54   M. Harris & G. Moran, *Reshaping Religious Education.* (Louisville, KY: Westminster/John Knox Press, 1998), p. 36.
55   G. Moran, *Showing How: The Act of Teaching.* (Valley Forge, PA: Trinity Press International, 1997), p. 112.
56   Ibid, pp. 114, 116.
57   Ibid, p. 117.
58   Ibid, p. 124.
59   Ibid, p. 125.
60   Ibid, p. 129.
61   Ibid, p. 133.
62   Ibid, p. 137.
63   Ibid, p. 144.
64   Ibid, p. 145.
65   Ibid, p. 145.
66   G. Moran, *Interplay,* (Winona: St. Mary's Press, 1981).
67   G. Moran, *Showing How: The Act of Teaching,* (Valley Forge: PA: Trinity Press International, 1997).
68   Ibid, p. 196.
69   E. Durkheim, *Moral Education,* (New York: Free Press, 1900), p. 3.
70   Ibid, pp. 18-19.
71   Ibid, p. 120.
72   G. Moran, *Showing How: The Act of Teaching,* (Valley Forge, PA: Trinity Press International, 1997), p. 198
73   J. Piaget, *The Moral Development of the Child,* (New York: Collier Press, 1962), p. 13. (Original work published 1932).

74   Ibid, p. 323.

75   G. Moran, *Interplay*, (Winona: St. Mary's Press, 1981), p. 123.

76   G. Moran, 1983, p. 73.

77   Ibid, p. 74,

78   Ibid, p. 88.

79   C. Gilligan, *In a Different Voice: Women's Conception of the Self and Morality*, (Cambridge, MA: Harvard University Press, 1977)

80   G. Moran, *Interplay*, (Winona: St. Mary's Press, 1981), p. 125.

81   C. Gilligan, *In A Different Voice: Women's Conception of the Self and Morality*, (Cambridge, MA: Harvard University Press, 1977), p. 498.

82   G. Moran, *Interplay*, (Winona: St. Mary's Press, 1981).

83   Ibid, p. 91.

84   Ibid, p. 91.

85   Ibid, p. 101.

86   Ibid, p. 97.

87   Ibid, p. 101.

88   G. Moran, *No Ladder to the Sky*, (San Francisco: Harper & Row, 1987a)

89   Ibid, p. 167.

90   Ibid, p. 5.

91   P. Devitt, *How Adult is Adult Religious Education?* (Dublin: Veritas, 1991), p. 273

92   G. Moran, 'Moral Education: Friend or Foe of Christian Education?' 1986, p. 95.

93   G. Moran, *No Ladder to the Sky*, p. 171.

94   Ibid, p. 171.

95   G. Moran, 'Moral Education', p. 97.

96   Ibid, p. 98.

97   G. Moran, *No Ladder to the Sky*, 1987.

98   Ibid, p. 14.

99   Ibid, p. 15.

100 G. Moran, *Showing How: The Act of Teaching*, (Valley Forge: Trinity Press International, 1997).

101 G. Moran, *No Ladder to the Sky*, 1987, p. 75.

102 Ibid, p. 75.

103 Ibid, p. 93.

104 Ibid, p. 85.

105 Ibid, p. 95.

106 G. Moran, *Showing How: The Act of Teaching*, (Valley Forge: Trinity Press International, 1997), p. 206.

107   Ibid, p. 209.
108   Ibid, p. 213.
109   1996, p. 140
110   Ibid, p. 216
111   Ibid, p. 216
112   Ibid, p. 217.
113   Ibid, p. 218.
114   G. Moran, *A Grammar of Responsibility*, (New York: Crossroad, 1996).
115   Ibid, p. 35.
116   Ibid, p. 35.
117   Ibid, p. 44.

Chapter 3

1   G. Moran, *Religious Body*, (New York: Seabury Press, 1974), p. 150.
2   Ibid, p. 173.
3   G. Moran, *Interplay*, (Winona, Ma: St. Mary's Press, 1981), p. 15.
4   Ibid, p. 17.
5   Ibid, p. 159.
6   G.A. Coe, *A Social Theory of Religious Education*, (New York: Charles Scribner's Sons, 1917), p. 80.
7   C. Ellis Nelson, *Where Faith Begins*, (Atlanta, GA: John Knox Press, 1971), p. 38.
8   P.J. Palmer, *To Know As We are Known*, (New York: McGraw-Hill, 1983), p. xi.
9   G. Moran, 'Understanding Religion and Being Religious', 1992. *PACE*, 21, 249-252.
10   C. Ellis Nelson, *Where Faith Begins*, (Atlanta, Ga: John Knox Press, 1972).
11   J.H. Westerhoff, *Will Our Children Have Faith?*, (New York: The Seabury Press, 1976).
12   J.H. Westerhoff & G. Kennedy Neville, *Generation to Generation*, (New York: The Pilgrim Press, 1974).
13   B. Marthaler, 'Socialization as a model for catechetics' in P. O'Hare (Ed.), *Foundations of Religious Education*. (New York: Paulist Press, pp. 64-90).
14   Ibid, p. 40.
15   Ibid, p. 65.
16   Ibid, p. 165.

17   John H. Westerhoff & G. Kennedy Neville, *Generation to Generation,* (New York: The Pilgrim Press, 1974), p. 41.

18   Ibid, p. 46.

19   B. Marthaler, 'Socialization as a model for catechetics' in P. O'Hare (Ed.), *Foundations of Religious Education.* (New York: Paulist Press, 1978), pp. 64-90.

20   J.H. Westerhoff, *Will Our Children Have Faith?* (New York: The Seabury Press, 1976), p. 23.

21   M. Harris & G. Moran, *Reshaping Religious Education.* (Louisville, Ky: Westminster John Knox Press, 1998), p. 30.

22   G. Moran, 'Understanding religion and being religious.' (1992). *PACE,* 21, p. 251.

23   J.H. Westerhoff & G. Kennedy Neville, *Generation to Generation,* (New York: The Pilgrim Press, 1974), p. 30.

24   Ibid, p. 43.

25   G. Moran, *Interplay,* (Winona, Ma: St. Mary's Press, 1981), p. 73.

26   Ibid, p. 73.

27   Ibid, p. 74.

28   J.S. Dunne, *The Way of all the Earth,* (Notre Dame: University of Notre Dame Press, 1978).

29   G. Moran, 'Religious Education after Vatican II' in D. Etroymson and J. Raines (Eds.) *Open Catholicism: The Tradition at its best,* (Collegeville, MN: The Liturgical Press, 1997), p. 156.

30   Ibid, p. 160.

31   National Conference of Catholic Bishops, *Sharing the Light of Faith,* (National Catechetical Directory for Catholics of the United States). (Washington, DC: United States Catholic Conference). #210.

32   G. Moran, 'Religious education after Vatican II' in D. Etroymson & J. Raines (Eds.). *Open Catholicism: The tradition at its best,* (Collegeville, MN: The Liturgical Press). p. 162.

33   G. Moran, 'Understanding Religion and Being Religious', PACE, 21, 1992. p. 252.

Chapter 4

1   G. Moran, *Showing How: The Act of Teaching,* (Valley Forge, PA: Trinity Press International, 1997), p. 158.

2   M. Sawin, *Family Enrichment with Family Clusters,* (Valley Forge, PA: Judson Press, 1979), p. 18.

3   L.A. Cremin, 'The Family as Educator: Some comments on the

recent historiography' in H.J. Leighter (Ed.) *The Family as Educator,* (New York: Teachers' College Press, 1974), p. 86.

4   Ibid, p. 86.

5   M. Harris, 'Art and Religious Education: A Conversation', *Religious Education,* 83, 1988. p. 463.

6   Ibid, p. 464.

7   G. Moran, *Showing How: The Act of Teaching,* (Valley Forge, PA: Trinity Press International, 1997), p. 156.

8   G. Moran, *No Ladder to the Sky,* (San Francisco: Harper & Row, 1987), p. 13.

9   G. Moran, *Showing How: The Act of Teaching,* (Valley Forge, PA: Trinity Press International, 1997), p. 157.

10   Ibid, p. 157.

11   G. Moran, *Religious Education Development,* (Minneapolis, MN: Winston Press, 1983), p. 165.

12   M. Sawin, *Family Enrichment with Family Clusters,* (Valley Forge, PA: Judson Press, 1979), p. 13.

13   H.J. Leichter, 'Some Perspectives on the Family as Educator' in H.J. Leichter, (Ed.), *The Family as Educator,* (New York: Teachers' College Press, 1974), p. 1.

14   Ibid, p. 1.

15   M. Harris, *The Faith of Parents,* (Mahwah, NJ: Paulist Press, 1991).

16   V. Satir, *Peoplemaking,* (Palo Alto, CA: Science & Behavior Books, 1972), pp. 21, 24.

17   M. Harris, *The Faith of Parents,* (Mahwah, NJ: Paulist Press, 1991), p. 46.

18   H.J. Leichter, 'Some Perspectives on the Family as Educator' in H.J. Leichter, (Ed.), *The Family as Educator.* (New York: Teachers' College Press, 1974), p. 17.

19   M. Mead, *Culture and Commitment: A Study of the Generation Gap,* (Garden City, NJ: Doubleday, 1970).

20   H.J. Leichter, 'Some Perspectives on the Family as Educator' in H.J. Leichter (Ed.), *The Family as Educator,* (New York: Teachers' College Press, 1974), p. 19.

21   D. P. Irish, 'Sibling Interaction: A Neglected Aspect in Family Life Research' in J.R. Eshleman (Ed.), *Perspectives in Marriage and the Family,* (Boston: Allyn & Bacon, 1970), p. 554.

22   C. Davis & M. Northway, 'Siblings: Rivalry or relationship? *Bulletin of the Institute for Child Study,* 19, (3), pp. 10-13.

23   H.J. Leichter, 'Some Perspectives on the Family as Educator' in H.J. Leichter (Ed.), *The Family as Educator,* (New York: Teachers' College

Press, 1974), p. 19.

24 D. P. Irish, 'Sibling Interaction: A Neglected Aspect in Family Life Research' in J.R. Eshleman (Ed.), *Perspectives in Marriage and the Family*, (Boston: Allyn & Bacon, 1970), p. 557.

25 E. Cumming & W. Henry, *Growing Old: The Process of Disengagement*, (New York: Basic Books, 1961).

26 H.J. Leichter, 'Some Perspectives on the Family as Educator' in H.J. Leichter (Ed.), *The Family as Educator*, (New York: Teachers College Press, 1974), p. 22.

27 Pope John Paul II, *Familiaris Consortio: Apostolic Exhortation on the Role of the Christian Family in the Modern World*, (Boston: Pauline Books & Media, 1981), p. 59.

28 G. Moran, *Showing How: The Act of Teaching*, (Valley Forge, PA: Trinity Press International, 1997).

29 Ibid, p. 70.

30 G. Moran, *Education Toward Adulthood*, (New York: Paulist Press, 1979), p. 85.

31 M.S. Van Leeuwen, 'Re-Inventing the Ties that Bind' in H. Anderson, D. Browning, I. Evison & M.S. Van Leeuwen (Eds.), *The Family Handbook*, (Louisville, KY: Westminster/John Knox Press, 1996), p. 36.

32 G. Moran, *Education Toward Adulthood*, (New York: Paulist Press, 1979), p. 92.

33 G. Moran, *Showing How: The Act of Teaching*, (Valley Forge, PA: Trinity Press International, 1997), p. 104.

34 Ibid, p. 208.

35 E. Durkheim, *Moral Education*, (New York: Free Press, 1900).

36 R. N. Bellah, 'The Church as the Context for the Family' in K. Scott & M. Warren (Eds.), *Perspectives on Marriage*, (New York: Oxford University Press, 1987), p. 159.

37 Ibid, p. 163.

38 T. Inglis, *Moral Monopoly*, p. 189.

39 G. Moran, *Religious Education Development*, 1983, p. 97.

40 P. Philibert, 1975, p. 462

41 G. Moran, p. 97.

42 Ibid, p. 98.

43 Ibid, p. 105.

44 G. Moran, *Education Toward Adulthood*, (New York: Paulist Press, 1979), p. 61.

45 M. Harris, *The Faith of Parents*, (Mahwah, NJ: Paulist Press, 1991), p. 68.

46   G. Moran, *Religious Education as a Second Language*, (Birmingham, AL: Religious Education Press, 1989), p. 237.

Chapter 5

1   G. Moran, *Showing How: The Act of Teaching*, (Valley Forge, PA: Trinity Press International, 1997), p. 175.

2   T. Sizer, *Horace's School*, (Boston: Houghton Mifflin, 1992), p. 11.

3   R. S. Peters, *Education and the Education of Teachers*, (Boston: Routledge & Kegan Paul, 1977).

4   H. Kliebard, *The Struggle for the American Curriculum, 1893-1958*, (Boston: Routledge & Kegan Paul, 1986), p. 254.

5   G. Moran, *Interplay*, (Winona, MN: St. Mary's Press, 1981).

6   Ibid, p. 43.

7   L. A. Cremin, *Public Education*, (New York: Basic Books, 1976).

8   Ibid, p. 3.

9   Ibid, pp. 74-75.

10   G. Moran, *Showing How: The Act of Teaching*, (Valley Forge, PA: Trinity Press International, 1997), p. 170.

11   Ibid, p. 170.

12   E. Brann, *Paradoxes of Education in a Republic*, (Chicago: University of Chicago Press, 1979), pp. 16-17.

13   G. Moran, *Education Toward Adulthood*, (New York: Paulist Press, 1979), p. 45.

14   Ibid, p. 47.

15   J. Dewey, *Democracy and Education*, (New York: Free Press, 1966. Original work published in 1908).

16   G. Moran, *Interplay*, (Winona, MN: St. Mary's Press, 1981), p. 69.

17   S. Rothman, *Woman's Proper Place*, (New York: Basic Books, 1976), p. 57.

18   G. Moran, *Interplay*, (Winona, MN: St. Mary's Press, 1981), p. 71.

19   G. Moran, *No Ladder to the Sky*, (San Francisco: Harper & Row, 1987), p. 77.

20   Ibid, p. 78.

21   Ibid, p. 79.

22   G. Moran, *Showing How: The Act of Teaching*, (Valley Forge, PA: Trinity Press International, 1997), p. 176.

23   E. Boyer, *High School: A Report on Secondary Education in America*, (New York: Harper & Row, 1973).

24   G. Moran, *Showing How: The Act of Teaching*, (Valley Forge, PA: Trinity Press International, 1997), p. 181.

25   Ibid, p. 181.

26   G. Moran, *Interplay*, (Winona, MN: St. Mary's Press, 1981), p. 74.

27   Ibid, p. 74.

28   P. Phenix, 'Religion in Public Education: Principles and Issues' in D. Engel (Ed.), *Religion in Public Education*, (New York: Paulist Press, 1974), p. 67.

29   G. Moran, *Interplay*, (Winona, MN: St. Mary's Press, 1981), p. 75.

30   R. M. Rilke, *Letters to a Young Poet*, (New York: W.W. Norton, 1934), p. 33.

31   M. Harris & G. Moran, *Reshaping Religious Education*, (Louisville, KY: Westminster/John Knox Press, 1998), p. 37.

32   G. Moran, *Showing How: The Act of Teaching*, (Valley Forge, PA: Trinity Press International, 1997), p. 202.

33   G. Moran, *No Ladder to the Sky*, (San Francisco: Harper & Row, 1987), p. 147.

34   Ibid, p. 160.

35   Ibid, p. 162.

36   Ibid, p. 162.

37   Ibid, p. 176.

38   Ibid, p. 183.

39   Ibid, p. 185.

40   G. Moran, *Showing How: The Act of Teaching*, (Valley Forge, PA: Trinity Press International, 1997), p. 210.

41   G. Moran, *Religious Education as a Second Language*, (Birmingham, AL: Religious Education Press, 1989), p. 170.

42   G. Moran, *Showing How: The Act of Teaching*, (Valley Forge, PA: Trinity Press International, 1997), p. 212.

43   Ibid, p. 214.

44   Ibid, p. 218.

Chapter 6

1   G. Moran, *Religious Body*, (New York: The Seabury Press, 1974), p. 109.

2   Ibid, p. 132.

3   Ibid, p. 113.

4   Ibid, p. 117.

5   Ibid, p. 121.

6   O. Brennan, *Cultures Apart: The Catholic Church and Contemporary Irish Youth*, (Dublin: Veritas, 2001), p. 183.

7   Ibid, p.132.

8   Ibid, p.135.

9   Ibid, p.139.

10 M. Harris, *Fashion Me A People*, (Louisville, KY: Westminster/John Knox Press, 1989), p. 75.

11 G. Moran, *Religious Body*, (New York: The Seabury Press, 1974).

12 G. Moran, *Interplay*, (Winona, MN: St. Mary's Press, 1981), pp. 101-105.

13 J. H. Westerhoff, *Will Our Children Have Faith?*, (New York: The Seabury Press, 1976), p. 52.

14 Ibid, p. 53.

15 Ibid, p. 54.

16 G. Moran, *Religious Education as a Second Language*, (Birmingham, Alabama: Religious Education Press, 1989), p. 144.

17 J. H. Westerhoff, *Will Our Children Have Faith?*, (New York: The Seabury Press, 1976), p. 64.

18 Ibid, p. 66.

19 M. Harris & G. Moran, *Reshaping Religious Education*, (Louisville, KY: Westminster/John Knox Press, 1998), p. 32.

20 G. Moran, *Religious Education as a Second Language*, (Birmingham, Al: Religious Education Press, 1989), p. 82.

21 M. Harris & G. Moran, *Reshaping Religious Education*, (Louisville, KY: Westminster/John Knox Press, 1998). P. 50.

22 G. Moran, *Showing How: The Act of Teaching*, (Valley Forge, PA: Trinity Press, International, 1997).

23 G. Moran, *Religious Education As A Second Language*, (Birmingham, Al: Religious Education Press, 1989), p. 150.

24 Ibid, p. 157.

25 G. Moran, *Showing How*, 1997. p. 206.

26 Ibid, p. 152.

27 M. Harris, *Fashion Me A People*, 1989, pp. 144-145.

28 Ibid, p. 148.

29 Ibid, p. 150.

30 Ibid, p. 152.

31 Ibid, p. 153.

32 G. Moran, *Showing How*, p. 195.

33 G. Moran, *Religious Education As A Second Language*, (1979), p. 177.

34 G. Moran, 1989, p. 183.

35 G. Moran, *Interplay*. (Winona, MN: St. Mary's Press, 1981), p. 115.

36 Ibid, p. 115.

37   G. Moran, *Religious Education As A Second Language*, (Birmingham, AL: Religious Education Press, 1989), p. 117.

38   L. Girzaitis, 'The Mature Christian Adult' in *Agenda for the 90s: Forging the Future of Adult Religious Education*, (Ed) N. Parent, (Washington, DC: Department of Education, United States Catholic Conference, 1988).

39   E. E. Whitehead & J.D Whitehead, *Christian Life Patterns*, (Garden City, NY: Doubleday, 1979).

40   J. Schaefer, 'Tensions between Adult Growth and Church Authority' in *Christian Adulthood*, (Ed) N. Parent, (Washington, DC: United States Catholic Conference, 1982).

41   Ibid, p. 22.

42   Ibid, p. 27.

43   J. Bacik, 'The Challenge of Christian Maturity', in *Educating for Christian Maturity*, (Ed) N. Parent, (Washington, DC: Department of Education, United States Catholic Conference, 1990).

44   Ibid, p. 7.

45   G. Moran, *Religious Education Development*, (Minneapolis, MN: Winston Press, 1983).

46   Ibid, p. 153.

BIBLIOGRAPHY

Bacik, J., 'The Challenge of Christian Maturity' in N. Parent (ed.), *Educating for Christian Maturity*, Washington, DC: Department of Education, United States Catholic Conference, 1990.

Bailyn, B., *Education in the Forming of American Society*, New York: Vintage Books, 1960.

Barker, K., *Religious Education, Catechesis and Freedom*, Birmingham, Alabama: Religious Education Press, 1981.

Barzun, J. & Graff, H., *The Modern Researcher*, Boston: Houghton Mifflin, 1992.

Bellah, R. N., 'The Church as the Context for the Family' in K. Scott & M. Warren (eds), *Perspectives on Marriage*, New York: Oxford University Press, 2000.

Boyer, E., *High School: A report on secondary education in America*, New York: Harper & Row, 1983.

Boys, M.C., 'Religious education: A map of the field' in M.C. Boys (ed.), *Education for Citizenship and Discipleship*, New York: Pilgrim Press, 1989.

Brann, E., *Paradoxes of Education in a Republic*, Chicago: University of Chicago Press, 1979.

Brennan, O., *Cultures Apart: The Catholic Church and Contemporary Irish Youth*, Dublin: Veritas, 2001.

Broudy, H.,'Between the Yearbooks' in J. Soltis (ed.), *Philosophy and Education*, Chicago: National Society for the Study of Education, 1981.

Bushnell, H., *Christian Nurture*, New Haven: Yale University Press, 1967 [1861].

Coe, G.A., *A Social Theory of Religious Education*, New York: Charles Scribner's Sons, 1917.

Cooley, C. H., *Social Organization: A study of the larger mind*, New York: Shocken, 1962 [1909].

Cremin, L.A., 'The Family as Educator: Some Comments on the Recent Historiography' in H.J. Leighter (ed.), *The Family as Educator*, New York: Teachers' College Press, 1974.

Cremin, L.A., *Public Education*, New York: Basic Books, 1976.

Crump Miller, R., *The Theory of Christian Education Practice*, Birmingham, Alabama: Religious Education Press, 1980.

Cumming, E., & Henry, W., *Growing Old: The Process of Disengagement*, New York: Basic Books, 1961.

Davis, C., & Northway, M., 'Siblings – Rivalry or Relationship?', *Bulletin of the Institute for Child Study*, 19:3, 1957, 8.

Devitt, P.M., *How Adult is Adult Religious Education?*, Dublin: Veritas, 1991.

Devitt, P.M., *That You May Believe*, Dublin: Dominican Publications, 1992.

Dewey, J., *Democracy and Education*, New York: Free Press, 1966.

Dunne, J.S., *The Way of All the Earth*, Notre Dame: University of Notre Dame Press, 1978.

Durka G., & Smith, J., *Family Ministry*, San Francisco: Harper & Row, 1980.

Durkheim, E., *Moral Education*, New York: Free Press, 1900.

Egan, K., *Educational Development*, New York: Oxford, 1979.

Elias, J.L., 'The Christian Family as Moral Educator: Possibilities and limitations' in G. Durka & J. Smith (ed.), *Family Ministry*, San Francisco: Harper & Row, 1980.

Elias, J.L. & Merriam, S., *Philosophical Foundations of Adult Religious Education*, Malabar, Florida: Kreiger Publishing Company, 1980.

Elliot, H.S., *Can Religious Education be Christian?*, New York: Macmillan, 1940.

Ellis Nelson, C., *Where Faith Begins*, Atlanta, GA: John Knox Press, 1971.

Flannery, A., *Pastoral Constitution on the Church in the Modern World: Gaudium et Spes*, Dublin: Dominican Publications, 1981.

Fowler, J., *Stages of Faith*, San Francisco: Harper & Row, 1981.

Fraile, G., 'History of philosophy', *New Catholic Encyclopedia*, II, New York: McGraw-Hill, 1967.

Francis, L.J., Astley, J & Robbins, M. (eds), *The Fourth R For The Third Millennium*, Dublin: Lindisfarne Books, 2001.

Girzaitis, L., 'The Mature Christian Adult' in N. Parent (ed.), *Agenda for the 90s: Forging the Future of Adult Religious Education*, Washington, DC: Department of Education, United States Catholic Conference, 1988.

Groome, T.H., *Christian Religious Education*, San Francisco: Harper & Row, 1980.

Groome, T.H., *Sharing Faith: A Comprehensive Approach to Religious Education and Pastoral Ministry: The Way of Shared Praxis*, San Francisco: Harper & Row, 1991.

Groome, T.H., *Educating for Life*, Allen, Texas: Thomas More, 1998.

Harris, M., 'Art and Religious Education: A conversation', *Religious Education*, 83, 3, 1988.

Harris, M., *Fashion Me A People: Curriculum in the Church*, Louisville, Kentucky: Westminster/John Knox Press, 1989.

Harris, M., *The Faith of Parents*, Mahwah, New Jersey: Paulist Press, 1991.

Harris, M., & Moran, G., *Reshaping Religious Education*, Louisville, Kentucky: Westminster/John Knox Press, 1998.

Hauerwas, S., 'The Family as a School for Character' in K. Scott & M. Warren (ed.), *Perspectives on Marriage*, New York: Oxford University Press, 2000.

Inglis, T., *Moral Monopoly: The Rise and Fall of the Catholic Church in Modern Ireland*, Dublin: University College Dublin Press, 1998.

Irish, D.P., 'Sibling interaction: A neglected aspect in family life research' in J. Ross Eshleman (ed.), *Perspectives in Marriage and the Family*, Boston: Allyn and Bacon, 1970.

Kaplan, A., *The Conduct of Inquiry: Methodology for Behavioural Science*. New Brunswick: Transaction Publishers, 1998.

Kliebard, H., *The Struggle for the American Curriculum, 1893-1958*, Boston: Routledge and Kegan Paul, 1986.

Lane, D., *Religious Education and the Future*, Mahwah, NJ: Paulist Press, 1986.

Leichter, H.J., 'Some Perspectives on the Family as Educator' in Hope Jensen Leichter (ed.), *The Family as Educator*, New York: Teachers College Press, 1974.

Marthaler, B., 'A Discipline in Quest of an Identity', *Horizons*, 68, 2, 1973.

Marthaler, B., 'Toward a Revisionist Model in Catechetics', *The Living Light*, 13:3, 1976.

Marthaler, B., 'Socialization as a Model for Catechetics' in P. O'Hare (ed.), *Foundations of Religious Education*, New York: Paulist Press, 1978.

Mead, M., *Culture and Commitment: A Study of the Generation Gap*, Garden City, New York: Doubleday, 1970.

Moran, G., *Design for Religion*, New York: Herder & Herder, 1971.

Moran, G., 'The intersection of religion and education', *Religious Education*, LXIX, 5, 1974a.

Moran, G., *Religious Body*, New York: The Seabury Press, 1974.

Moran, G., 'Two languages of religious education', *The Living Light*, 14, 1977.

Moran, G., 'Where now, what next?' in P. O'Hare (ed.), *Foundations of Religious Education*, Mahwah, New Jersey: Paulist Press, 1978.

Moran, G., *Education Toward Adulthood*, New York: Paulist Press, 1979.

Moran, G., 'Parish Models of Education' in Maria Harris Winona (ed.), *The DRE reader: A Sourcebook in Education and Ministry*, Minnesota: St Mary's Press, 1980.

Moran, G., *Interplay*, Winona, Minnesota: St Mary's Press, 1981.

Moran, G., 'From Obstacle to Modest Contributor: Theology in Religious Education' in N.H. Thompson, *Religious Education and Theology*, Birmingham, Alabama: Religious Education Press, 1982.

Moran, G., *Religious Education Development*, Minneapolis, Minnesota: Winston Press, 1983.

Moran, G. 'Moral Education: Friend or Foe of Christian Education' in Dermot A. Lane, *Religious Education and The Future*, Mahwah, New Jersey: Paulist Press, 1986.

Moran, G., *No Ladder to the Sky*, San Francisco: Harper & Row, 1987a.

Moran, G. 'Religious education' in M. Eliade (ed.), *Encyclopedia of Religion*, 12, New York: Macmillan, 1987b.

Moran, G., 'Of a Kind and to a Degree: A Roman Catholic Perspective' in M. Mayr (ed.), *Does the Church Really Want Religious Education.*, Birmingham, Alabama: Religious Education Press, 1988.

Moran, G., *Religious Education as a Second Language*, Birmingham, Alabama: Religious Education Press, 1989.

Moran, G., 'Understanding Religion and Being Religious', *PACE*, 21, 1992, 249-252.

Moran, G., 'Two Languages of Religious Education' in J. Astley & L.J. Francis (eds), *Critical Perspectives on Christian Education*, Leonminster, Herefordshire: Gracewing, 1994.

Moran, G., *A Grammar of Responsibity*, New York: The Crossroad Publishing Company, 1996.

Moran, G., 'Religious Education after Vatican II' in by D. Etroymson & J. Raines (eds), *Open Catholicism: The Tradition at its Best*, Collegeville, Minnesota: The Liturgical Press, 1997a.

NEW DIRECTIONS IN RELIGIOUS EDUCATION

Moran, G., *Showing How: The Act of Teaching*, Valley Forge, PA: Trinity Press International, 1997b.

Moran, G., & Harris, M., *Reshaping Religious Education*, Louisville, Kentucky: Westminster/John Knox Press, 1998.

National Conference of Catholic Bishops, *Sharing the Light of Faith, National Catechetical Directory for Catholics of the United States*, Washington, DC: United States Catholic Conference, 1979.

Nesbitt, E. 'Representing Faith Traditions in Religious Education: An Ethnographic Perspective' in L.J. Francis, J. Astley & M. Robbins (eds), *The Fourth R For The Third Millennium*, Dublin: Lindisfarne Books, 2001.

Newmann, F., & Oliver, D., 'Education and Community' in T. Sizer (ed.), *Religion and Public Education*, Boston: Houghton Mifflin, 1967.

Nichols, K. *Refracting the Light: Learning the Languages of faith*, Dublin: Veritas Publications, 1997.

Nicholson, J. P., 'A Critical Analysis of the Theological, Sociological, Education and Organizational Dimensions of Westerhoff's Socialization-Enculturation Paradigm', Doctoral dissertation, Fordham University, 1980, *Dissertation Abstracts International*, 41, 4670A-4671A.

Oakeshott, M., 'Learning and Teaching' in T. Fuller (ed.), *The Voice of Liberal Learning*, New Haven: Yale University Press, 1989.

O'Donnell, D., 'Insightful Evaluation: The Development of a Theory for the Evaluation of Educational Administrators', Doctoral dissertation, Fordham University, 1983, *Dissertation Abstracts International*, 43, 3772A.

Palmer P.J., *To Know As We Are Known*, New York: McGraw-Hill, 1983.

Parent, N., *Agenda for the 90s: Forging the Future of Adult Religious Education*, Department of Education, United States Catholic Conference, 1988.

Peters, R.S., *Education and the Education of Teachers*, Boston: Routledge and Kegan Paul, 1977.

Phenix, P.H., *Realms of Meaning*, New York: McGraw-Hill, 1964.

Phenix, P., 'Religion in Public Education: Principles and Issues' in D. Engel (ed.), *Religion in Public Education*, New York: Paulist Press, 1974.

Piaget, J., *The Moral Judgment of the Child*, New York: Collier Press, 1962.

Pope John Paul II, *Familiaris Consortio: Apostolic Exhortation on the Role of the Christian Family in the Modern World*, Boston: Pauline Books and Media, 1981.

Rilke, R.M., *Letters to a Young Poet*, New York: W.W. Norton & Co., 1934.

Rothman, S., *Woman's Proper Place*, New York: Basic Books, 1978.

Satir, V., *Peoplemaking*, Palo Alto, Calif.: Science and Behavior Books, 1972.

Sawin, M., *Family Enrichment With Family Clusters*, Valley Forge, Pa.: Judson Press, 1979.

Schaefer, J., 'Tensions Between Adult Growth and Church Authority' in N. Parent, *Christian Adulthood*, Department of Education, United States Catholic Conference, 1982.

Scott, K., 'Communicative competence and religious education', *Lumen Vitae*, 35, 1, 1980, 75-96.

Scott, K., 'The Family, Feminism and Religious Education', *Religious Education*, 75, 3, 1980, 327-341.

Scott, K., 'Catechesis and Religious Education: Uncovering the Nature of Our Work', *PACE*, 12, 1981.

Scott, K., 'The Local Church as an Ecology of Human Development', *Religious Education*, 72, 2, 1981, 142-161.

Scott, K., 'Three Traditions of Religious Education', *Religious Education*, 79, 3, 1984, 323-339.

Scott, K., & Warren, M., *Perspectives on Marriage*, New York: Oxford University Press, 1993.

Scriven, M., 'Philosophical Inquiry Methods in Education' in R.M. Jaeger (ed.), *Complementary methods for research in education,* Washington, DC: American Educational Research Association, 1968.

Shelton Smith, H., *Faith and Nurture,* New York: Charles Scribner's Sons, 1950.

Sizer, T., *Horace's School,* Boston: Houghton Mifflin, 1992.

Towns, E.L., 'Method in Philosophic Inquiry for Christian Education', *Religious Education, 63,* 1972, 259-267.

Van Leeuwen, M. S., 'Re-inventing the Ties that Bind' in H. Anderson, D. Browning, I. Evison & M. Van Leeuwen (eds), *The Family Handbook,* Louisville, Kentucky: Westminster/John Knox Press, 1996.

Vigilanti, J.A., 'The autonomy of the student in higher education: An interdisciplinary examination of academic freedom in Catholic universities', *Doctoral Abstracts International,* 52, 868A, 1991.

Walsh, J.R., *Religion: The Irish Experience,* Dublin: Veritas, 2003.

Westerhoff, J.H., *Will Our Children Have Faith?,* New York: The Seabury Press, 1976.

Westerhoff, J.H., *Who are We?,* Birmingham, Alabama: Religious Education Press, 1978.

Westerhoff, J.H., & Kennedy Neville, G., *Generation to Generation,* New York: The Pilgrim Press, 1974.

Whitehead, E., & Whitehead, J., (19) *Christian Life Patterns,* New York: The Crossroad Publishing Company, 1996.